Contents

1. The Problem Discovered   7
2. The Forces of Dissolution   16
3. The Libraries   25
4. The Rise of Semi-Literacy   53
   Sample List of Institutions   59
   Sample List of Books Dispersed   73
   Notes   87
   Index   89

To the founders of the public
libraries of England and those
who uphold their ideals

1

The Problem Discovered

As I was walking down Sackville Street one fine spring day in 1985 I noticed a sign in the window of a bookshop, now no more, advertising BBC books for sale. Inside in the back of the shop was a large room containing, indeed, thousands of BBC books. But they were not remainders from the massive output of BBC Enterprises. The room was filled with books from the Library at Broadcasting House, the BBC headquarters, and the Langham Hotel opposite, which the BBC occupied for so many years.

I had recently been working on Orwell's radio scripts in the BBC's Written Archive Centre at Caversham, one of the most important archives for modern British history outside the Public Record Office, and here in this room in Sackville Street were books written by all the authors and broadcasters I had grown familiar with, who were working at the time George Orwell was broadcasting and before. Una Marson, the Jamaican poet, had worked with Orwell, and was well known to West Indian listeners. Here was the BBC's copy of her exceedingly rare volume of poems published in 1945. And so on.

Until this melancholy event the BBC's collection – its library archive, sound archive and scripts library – had formed an integrated whole unrivalled anywhere in the world. It stretched from the infancy of radio broadcasting in the early twenties right through to television and the present day. People did broadcasts, and if they wrote books, or gave talks on books, these books were all to be found in the BBC Library, along with a fine technical collection and an unrivalled political section, dating back to the days when Guy Burgess ran their first Parliamentary programmes. Now this unique collection was broken beyond recall, without even an obituary in the press – no letter of protest, no formal announcement of the reason for the vandalism.

Unknown to me at the time, other significant dispersals had already taken place. They included the Brent Library scandal when 105,000 books were lost. There, paradoxically, the complex of reasons had included the need to focus on the interests of minorities and avoid racism: presumably Una Marson's poems would have been safe with them. A debate was going on within the library profession on the whole question of dispersals and conservation which culminated in a symposium at Loughborough in 1987 chaired by Lord Quinton, Chairman of the British Library Board, and a report by the British Library itself, *Selection for Survival: A Review of Acquisition and Retention Policies* (1989). This and the text of the symposium which was also published will be referred to here. But they were symptoms of what was happening, not an analysis of the problem.

Neither Lord Quinton nor any of the professionals involved saw things from the point of view of the reading public. And they were probably themselves unaware of the scale of what had been happening, not just in their own field of Public Libraries, which was bad enough, but across the whole spectrum of British Public and Institutional Libraries.

This book is about such events: a cultural catastrophe which has gathered pace and which, if not addressed by those in power, could do irreparable damage to our nation's literary heritage. In some cases, such as the BBC's, though damage has been done the library, surviving still, has critical mass and is usable. In the Brent case, and others I have discovered while writing this book, such as the specialist cotton library at New Mills, it is too late.

Libraries both public and institutional are disposing of books without any public debate, apart from a few over-heated outbursts in local newspapers and professional journals, forgotten as soon as read and never taken seriously. In the community as a whole there has been no awareness at all of what is happening. The context of this calm acquiescence is a rise in what I will call semi-literacy, which relies on the visual image and hardly at all on the printed word except as a medium of advertising, and genuinely cannot see what the problem is. And there are enemies within the system also. As Lord Quinton remarked at one point:

> Many books which my more ardent academic colleagues (and I too at the time) might have cheerfully consigned to the dustbin have been saved by the splendid professional retentiveness of librarians.[1]

Lord Quinton could never have imagined that in the columns of the *Library Association Record* in 1990 someone would suggest, only half jokingly as we shall see, that the librarian's motto should be 'When in Doubt, Chuck it Out'.

Visiting local bookshops at random, I came across more and more books that had come from libraries. The West Country, where I live, is a natural depository of books, carried down there by people who have retired from all over the country. These bookshops reflect more than local happenings. Their owners were also beginning to notice what was going on and commented on the changes that were making their business more difficult, for the books often had no dispersal markings on them. What guarantee was there that they had not been stolen?

Finding a book from one of the great libraries out on the loose without a cancellation stamp is a disquieting experience, especially when it comes from one of the older Universities. Ten years ago anyone finding such a book would have returned it if they could. Booksellers responded similarly. Even now one of the best-known West Country booksellers sends a standard letter to any institution if a book from its library comes into their possession without a dispersal stamp. The universal feeling used to be that such books belonged in the libraries they came from. Indeed in any civilised country it is difficult to see what other view could be held. The rise of semi-literacy in England has swept away all such certainties.

Within the last decade, the boom-and-slump Eighties, the

situation worsened. By the end of the Eighties there were so many library books in the shops and on market stalls (a mediaeval phenomenon that still survives in market towns in Devon and elsewhere) that it was clear to anyone that a new situation had arisen. In 1990 there was a breakthrough in public consciousness when entire libraries were being closed in the Midlands and other parts of Britain, and other libraries were cutting back on new books, or freezing purchase grants.

Actual closures naturally caused concern. The local authorities who approved such acts seemed unaware of the immense capital sums, not to mention years of work, that had gone into creating these libraries since their foundation in Victorian times, and their complete loss by the simple act of dispersal. Perhaps it was never explained to them. It is one sign of the rise of semi-literacy that the descendants of the nineteenth-century civic worthies who took pride in the libraries they opened genuinely cannot see any problem in closing them down a hundred years later, or authorising the ruthless dispersal of their stocks built up during that period.

Among those who helped create the public library system in England were the benefactor Andrew Carnegie, whose libraries can be found from Ayr to Brentford, W.H. Smith, whose eponymous book chain still *is* bookselling for the average English man and woman, and Mr Gladstone. There is a splendid account of the struggle to bring literacy to the masses by one of the central figures of the time, now forgotten, Thomas Greenwood. The edition of his book I quote from here was published a hundred years ago, in 1891. It should be compulsory reading for every student attending a library school in Britain. It is: *Public Libraries: A History of the Movement and a Manual for the Organization and Management of Rate-Supported Libraries by Thomas Greenwood FRGS.*

Despite press coverage of closures and cut-backs, real and imagined, there was no mention of the dispersals, or of the more worrying phenomenon of the general dissolution of libraries that seemed from local evidence to be taking place. I thought it worth checking to see just how far this had gone.

To get a wider picture than I had obtained from the local

PUBLIC LIBRARIES:

A HISTORY OF THE MOVEMENT AND A MANUAL FOR THE

ORGANIZATION AND MANAGEMENT

OF

RATE-SUPPORTED LIBRARIES.

BY

THOMAS GREENWOOD, F.R.G.S.,

AUTHOR OF "MUSEUMS AND ART GALLERIES," "EMINENT NATURALISTS," ETC.

FOURTH EDITION, REVISED AND BROUGHT UP TO DATE.

Twelfth Thousand.

CASSELL & COMPANY, LIMITED:

LONDON, PARIS, & MELBOURNE.

1891.

bookshops I made special journeys to various places, and acquired every library book I came across, only restricting myself by not acquiring more than one book from each library. Within days it was obvious that the extent of the dissolution was every bit as great as I had at first suspected. I continued the search over six weeks in Bristol, Oxford, Swindon, London, Rochester, Brighton, Cambridge, Derby, Edinburgh and Exeter, where this book was written. About three hundred libraries were chosen. But as some of the books had been through more than one library, the actual figures that emerged were 260 books from 292 libraries. The number could easily have been doubled, and doubled again, in further trips, but what I had discovered was already enough to reveal the full horror of what was happening.

The first observation I was able to make when the books were gathered together was that, although almost all the press coverage had been about public libraries, since they were the focus of political controversy, only *c*. 20 per cent of the random sample of the libraries were public in any normal sense of the word. The largest category, about a third, was libraries of educational institutions, ranging from Oxford and Cambridge colleges down to 'amalgamated' teacher-training colleges whose 'old-fashioned' libraries were deemed mostly redundant in the face of new teaching theories. (The most notorious of these theories is the 'real books' method of learning. The method clearly does not extend to the keeping of too many of the 'real books' themselves.)

The amount of material that came to hand, and the urgency of bringing home to the public what was happening, even if possible *stopping* what was happening, suggested the form of this book. The sample list of libraries at the end shows how serious the phenomenon is and forestalls criticism of the kind I have already heard: 'The situation is wildly exaggerated. Only a handful of libraries are involved. Brent was a freak.' The sample list of books is equally important, for it disarms criticisms of the kind: 'The books involved are obsolete and the shelf space is needed for more modern colourful illustrated books', or 'Things like this have always been going on', or 'We only get rid of popular novels when the rush is over'.

Like finds at an archaeological site, each book listed here is an object that speaks for itself. It has been discarded as worthless for any library purpose, like an old shoe or damaged pot in a mediaeval rubbish tip. These books speak of betrayal – of betrayal of the ideals of a public library system, of the system of higher education and the education of our teachers, and, at the highest level, of gifts and endowments and the historical integrity of collections that were at the heart of the country's literary culture. And in a country whose language has become the world's *lingua franca* its literary culture *is* its culture. The emergence of semi-literacy in England of all places, in ways which would make other civilised nations shrink in disgrace, is central to the catastrophe, and will be described alongside the accounts of the libraries and books themselves.

*

The list of libraries will come as a shock to anyone who is unaware of what has been happening. Professional organisations like the Library Association have been conscious of the problem, and have issued a useful policy directive on the dispersal of valuable books. But even those who discard books forget that they exist in the real world and that the booksellers sell to real customers. An act of dispersal made in secrecy, often reluctantly at the behest of political masters, immediately becomes as public as the shelves of the local bookshop. And the more valuable the book the greater the ultimate scandal, for it will probably end up on the shelves of libraries in other parts of the world where the literary culture of England is still prized.

Those who have to make the decision whether to keep or discard are often people who have spent their lives among books. They are obliged to make decisions that go against the grain. Unhappily there is a new breed of librarian who takes a different view, epitomised in the motto I have quoted 'If in Doubt, Chuck it Out'. One librarian who still clung to the old ideals remarked:

The anguish of the library book-despoiler is very real, and the mutual support, whether or not your decision is seconded, is a great relief. Book disposal is vandalism of the highest order; the agony and the responsibility need to be shared. One-in one-out is for the supermarkets, not the community's cultural and intellectual repository![2]

The new breed is epitomised by the library manager at Marylebone Public Library who remarked:

Librarians who get too attached to their stock are doing the profession no favours. Our motto should be 'If in Doubt, Chuck it Out'. There should be no science to book disposal. We do not need complex check lists and guidelines for action. These may have been possible in the days of full staffing and adequate resources. But we no longer have the luxury to sit and ponder the merits of every item of stock.[3]

The use of the word 'profession' is odd. Even odder is a profession that would take such a motto. This was the kind of language that used to be attributed to the sharper end of the second-hand book world. Now the situation is reversed.

Another librarian, remarking on the logistics of dispersals, said:

There is a clear difference between library stock disposals and the second-hand book trade. The latter accepts shelf-life [i.e. that books will be available in the same place for a reasonable period of time] as part of the process, the librarian-disposer wants quick clearance.[4]

And it would seem that in this matter of dispersals the book 'trade' is a more honourable calling than the so-called library 'profession', at least as it is carried on by its present *avant garde*.

I mention this struggle within the 'profession' because whenever some particularly disgraceful scandal occurs, such as the New Mills dispersal, or the dispersal at Brent, there will always be a tendency to blame the 'professional' involved. And since each book here can be traced back to those whose decision it was to discard, it is important to emphasise that no personal blame is implied, and that the *responsibility* for what occurred is not his necessarily, but of those who employed him. Many librarians have written in to protest at what has been happening and there has been a good deal of debate behind closed doors; but, as will be shown here, the ultimate explanation is the rise of semi-literacy and the acceptance of it by the modern descendants of the great Victorians. Let us hope that librarians of the right stuff (to use a Victorian expression) will find arguments here to take to those who provide the funds to *demand*, not ask, that funds be provided to stop unnecessary dispersals, and that space be acquired for storage – no longer difficult in the worst property slump since the war.

2

The Forces of Dissolution

Although dispersals have been made from every library on the list at the end of this book – and, as has been remarked, the list could have been extended to twice its size or more by further random sampling – it is obvious that the dissolutions took place for different reasons, some less culpable than others. One reason often given for the dispersal of books is their *appearance*, and not their physical state – any shabbiness or indication that people might actually be reading them – but the visual appeal of their dust-jacket design. One librarian remarked:

> I *have* known colleagues gleefully purging their shelves by the linear metre and filling skips by the ton often in the cause of some new fad or fashion such as trying 'face-on' display...[5]

'Face-on' display is the method of arranging books so that the dust-jacket is seen face-on as it would be in bookshop display. Another librarian, a keen proselytiser of the new ways, said:

> What is needed is a lean, muscular, high-turnover stock presented in attractive and imaginative ways...Nothing *looks* worse than bays stuffed full of unappealing books [my italics].

Books have been called many things in their time, but not 'lean and muscular'. And the reason they seem 'unappealing' is that they are not visually attractive. It is an old saying that you cannot tell a book by its cover. One of the tenets of the semi-literate is that not only can you tell a book by the picture on its cover but there should be a lot more pictures like it inside, and not much else.

Librarians who think this way, and who dispose of books by the skipful because they do not look appealing enough for 'face-on' display, have the excuse that almost all publishers regard the dust-jacket as the main way of selling a book. Books can be sold on their jackets to impulse buyers who may well not read more than a few pages once they have bought them.

It is obvious that if disposals continued by the ton for such crude reasons, then semi-literacy would be the inevitable consequence, because, in simple terms, the libraries would loose their critical mass. That is, the underlying holdings of serious reference works, older classics, local history and other books of more than ephemeral interest would fall to such a low level that most readers' questions and serious enquiries could not be answered without outside help.

It is important to realise that serious books of this kind, which form the backbone of the libraries and were first laid down by the Victorians, are most often those which are not taken out or 'issued' at all. Even when nominally on loan shelves, as in libraries in which loan and reference stocks are placed on the same shelves, these kinds of book are not borrowed but referred to. People come to the library with specific queries which are answered by reference then and there. In University libraries this is well understood, and there are often systems that allow the librarian to know when a book is not on its shelf because it is being used in the library. The loss of this basic perspective produces the worst problems and the biggest scandal. A senior librarian mulling over his difficulties said:

> Our concern is with that huge category of stock which is not issuing well and which fills our valuable storage space: the nineteenth-century biographies; the classics of politics and philosophy; the long journal runs; the multi-volume histories; the 'complete' works; the novels, plays and studies of and by yesterday's men and women; the giant topographical histories – the accumulated cultural and

historical heritage that lies heavily on the stacks and on the reference shelves.[7]

This man went on to describe how the entire lot had been dumped. His statement is almost a classic of philistinism. To take one example only. The 'giant topographical histories' were the result of immense labour. Anyone researching local history in a library, not finding such books, and not knowing of their existence, could embark on exhaustive duplication of work already done before. The very purpose of the library is defeated.

The result, when his depredations had been completed, was a library no doubt visually 'appealing' in the highest degree but entirely useless and without critical mass of any kind. It is worth quoting here from a speech made by Gladstone when he opened St Martin-in-the-Fields public library a hundred years ago, and a few words in answer by W.H. Smith who, incidentally, was of the opposite political persuasion: party politics were not involved in these vital matters then. Gladstone said:

> These libraries...they are all instruments with which a war is carried on. War against what? War against ignorance, war against brutality...How happy it is to see with what zeal and what promptitude all over the country the working population have exhibited their readiness to take advantage of the opportunities when once afforded them. I express to you the most earnest desire of my heart to be that prosperity and success in social and moral improvement may attend increasingly from year to year the progress of this library.[8]

Smith answered:

> As Mr Gladstone has pointed out, in the last few years progress has been far more rapid because improved education has created in all classes of the community an increased desire and appetite for literature which did not formerly exist, and that can only be supplied by means of such public libraries in which we are now met.[9]

The contrast between these two extracts and the rank philistin-ism exhibited in the previous quotation could hardly be greater. Elsewhere in his speech Gladstone specifically referred to the long runs of periodicals in the library as being of interest to him as he could not keep them in his own library. Added salt in the wound is that one of the books in the list that follows is taken from the collection which was around Gladstone as he spoke, and that another is one actually given to a library by his trustees.

*

The most obvious reason why there is a greater concern with visual images than with the printed word may be thought to be the emergence of the new media – film, television and even the computer. It was for this reason that the BBC's dispersal of a large part of its library holdings was so poignant. There is some truth in this simple account of the rise of semi-literacy, but in fact it is a complex phenomenon. Before looking in more detail at the different kinds of library on the list it is worth examining some of the less obvious causes.

The first has been the slow change-over from travel by train to travel by car. The Victorians spent countless hours on trains and passed many of them reading books. W.H. Smith owed no small part of his fortune to the stalls he had placed on every station platform, many of which not only offered a full range of books and papers but operated lending libraries. Literacy was confirmed as the cornerstone of everyone's life by such chance factors as the transformation of the country by rail travel. People who travel by rail still read an immense amount. Indeed there are those who rely to such an extent on the time they gain for reading on trains that travelling by road is not an option. In America, with its vast distances, plane travel plays a much larger part in people's lives than in Britain, and this may even be a contributory cause of the greater general literacy that is found in America today. There airport bookstalls play the role of the railway bookstalls of Victorian Britain and they carry a far wider range of books than those in England's railway stations today.

The overall loss of reading time, and even the loss of the reading habit as it was known to earlier generations, should not be underestimated. The effect on the administrative classes was greatest of all. Despite her lauding of other Victorian virtues, Mrs Thatcher was known for her un-Victorian dislike of rail travel and was typical of those of her rising generation in placing a car high on her list of social desiderata and symbols of prosperity. If this resulted in a great loss of reading time when compared with her Victorian predecessors such as Gladstone, and an equivalent change of attitude, then the results have been striking. They spread to the Conservative Party's own library where they were in marked contrast to the public image created by her backing of the new British Library buildings, as we shall see shortly.

The overall effect on administrators and senior figures generally, as far as concerns their reading habits and the amount they read, has been great. Another factor which has reinforced this and which has hardly been remarked on in this context is the telephone. Anyone who researches in the Public Record Office, the BBC archives or any other great collection, cannot fail to notice the impact of the telephone in reducing general literacy, particularly at levels just below the most senior. Files which before the war were lucid and precise, with everything stated simply in model letters and reports, become in the fifties and sixties thin and skimped with occasional notes 'for the file' covering actions taken after lengthy phone calls in which the actual decisions were made.

Historians of the future – assuming that the new teaching syllabus and the inclinations of the new wave of teachers from the teacher-training colleges with their 'lean and muscular' libraries allow the subject of history a place in England at all – will have difficulty in piecing together what actually influenced vital decisions. Those making the decisions have become in a precise sense semi-literate: they *can* read and write, it is just that they seldom do. Even their reports, which before the war would have been held together by close logic and the normal sense of what was being said, are now things of numbered paragraphs (the British Library report cited earlier has sections with triple numbers, such as 9.6.1, and even the conclusions of chapters have introductions) with no style or overall understanding at all. To this is added a rage for acronyms which has survived the ending of the war forty-five years ago, creating a sub-Orwellian world in which words are insensibly destroyed by being absorbed in outlandish cyphers.[10]

Whereas in Victorian England the provision of libraries was not seen as a matter of political contention, in modern England the political factor has operated directly in the closure and cut-backs of libraries. The worst offenders are almost always Councils controlled by extreme left factions engaged in what the present Chairman of the Conservative Party, Christopher Patten, has referred to as 'bleeding-stump politics'. And it is true that if, for example, there were a library catering specifically for the mentally retarded, this would be the first to be closed because it would create the greatest publicity. Unfortunately the Conservative Party itself helped set the tone for library disposals and helped not a little towards the rise of semi-literacy and, when controversy did arise, its political acceptability.

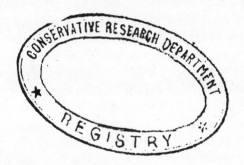

At the heart of the Conservative Party is its research Department, and at the heart of that department was its library. At some point early in Mrs Thatcher's tenure the conclusion was reached that this collection of volumes assembled over many decades was of no great use. Presumably its resources were thought to have been supplanted by those of the advertising agency that helped the Conservative Party to power. Having got the Party in, its research was thought to supersede, no doubt, any actual knowledge of political history beyond what was available in office memory.

It was decided to bring about the dissolution of the greater part of this library, and the library was offered for sale by Messrs Sotheby at one of the provincial salerooms they then owned, Sotheby's Taunton. I was present at the sale and bought a set of *Keesing's Contemporary Archives* which have proved invaluable, though I have used them with the usual misgivings that accompany the enjoyment of a benefit which has been denied to others. Presumably Conservative Central Office possessed another set, or got by somehow with occasional trips to Westminster Library. The bulk of the Collection was sold in mass lots contained in one or more tea-chests arranged in groups around a large room. Churchill's early books, treasured by earlier custodians of the Party's heritage, were thrown in with the rest. Whatever did not sell was, it is said, traded off from stalls at the next Party Conference.

Not surprisingly the threat of library dissolutions, especially those which librarians were claiming had been forced on them by government cut-backs, failed to get an immediate response from Mrs Thatcher's administration. Christopher Patten, who was then in charge of the Research Department, but is now in total control of the Party machine, will find it difficult to re-establish the library and its heritage, even supposing that the catalogues have been kept so that he knows what has been lost. He will once again have to rely on the advertising men, with their inimitable touch, rather than in-depth research by his own bright young men in the Research Department.

The advertising research teams will no doubt be equal to the task. They will identify and 'think through' the issues – or rather do the market analysis that substitutes for political thought – and create the slogans and policies in terms of the conditioned reflexes of the electorate which can be controlled by political advertising on the issues.

The picture of politics drawn here is not one that a literate Victorian would recognise. There are few public meetings now and fewer serious discussions in pamphlets, or even books, of a kind that would have made sense to a novelist like Disraeli, or a scholar like Gladstone, to both of whom the idea of a 'speech writer' or of an advertising agency to identify the issues would have been absurd. The scene is rather that portrayed in such modern masterworks as *Yes, Minister*, a key text of late-twentieth-century English political thought, and novels like Michael Dobbs's *House of Cards* – Mr Dobbs being appropriately enough, Deputy Chairman of Saatchi and Saatchi, the advertising agency, and a friend and colleague of Christopher Patten. And both these books pale before novels that contend for the mantle of Disraeli: those of Jeffrey Archer himself.

There is a direct cross-over between this fictional world of politics and semi-literacy, for these books have appeared on television and then sold many more copies in paperback as 'TV tie-ins'. The political semi-literacy implied is shown by the fact that the coverage they get is considerably more than that afforded to 'real' politics which is focused on the party political broadcasts preserved, like flies in amber, from earlier serious political coverage on radio and television. The public naturally turn to books of fiction, or televised versions of them, rather than to serious books. They will absorb the collected *Yes, Minister*, and its sequel the collected *Yes, Prime Minister*, in their entirety but not think of opening a real political text.

And yet there is still some vestige of genuine literacy in the works of Archer, Dobbs and the authors of *Yes, Minister*. Though they are contemptuously referred to as 'page turners', they are nevertheless texts and can engage the attention of those reading them, even developing patterns of thought which may affect the real world, as Disraeli's novels did in the last century. The difference being, of course, that in those days the phenomenon of semi-literacy did not exist and readers of Disraeli's or Thackeray's novels would neither mistake them for the real world, nor read them to the exclusion of all real political texts.

Beyond the page-turner are the real semi-literate books which are of another kind entirely. They perhaps owe something to the tabloid newspapers and colour supplements, as these have emerged in the post-war years, with their high illustrative content and minimal text. The books that follow this pattern are at first sight attractive, ideal for 'face-on' displays, and can even seem to have some serious purpose. But they are designed on quite different principles from literate books. There is no text that can be read, such as there is even in a children's comic. Instead they are designed to be 'read' in the following way. The book is opened at random. A picture or two is looked at. The 'extended captions' substituting for the old-fashioned text are read. The book is then opened at another random place and the process is repeated. Finally it is put down as boredom sets in and some other activity is engaged in. Perhaps the television is turned on (if it is not on already) or a colour supplement may be taken up, or an illustrated mail order catalogue browsed through.

People who have been conditioned to this kind of reading pattern and who still have the habit of frequenting their local library require similar fare there. Before long they are unable to digest anything else, even a 'page-turner'. It is to these people that the librarians are trying to appeal with their experiments in 'face-on' displays. They have to buy these books, which are not cheap, being printed usually in four colours on a lavish scale and accompanied by expensive 'hype' to bring them to the attention of the public. It is this kind of 'book' which has eaten away at budgets and corrupted the library staff more than any other.

These factors, the loss of reading time, the use of the telephone, the political dimension and the emergence of the specifically semi-literate book, together paint a background to the picture of the strange rise of semi-literate England. They should be borne in mind as we look at the final symptom of this 'strange rise': the dispersal of the libraries, and the libraries themselves caught in this downward spiral.

3

The Libraries

The sample libraries listed at the end are basically of three kinds.
First, there are the older libraries which were the forerunners
of the public libraries. Secondly, there are the public libraries
themselves. Lastly, there are the libraries at the colleges, ranging from Oxford and Cambridge to the most recent
amalgamations of teacher-training and technical colleges. I will
look at them briefly in turn and then at the remainder, which
are not without interest and include the little-known armed
forces libraries.

I made the choice at random, the sole criterion being that a
book had to have come from a library and have a recognisable
sign of its origin. The only time I considered the title of a book
was when I found a large number of books from the same library
together. I then chose one that was of interest for some other
reason. For example, a shop in London contained several hundred books from the Loughborough School of Librarianship.
There had been two schools of librarianship at Loughborough.
The one associated with the University was the one chosen to
survive. Books from the other college were dispersed,
presumably because they were duplicates. I chose the example
I did because it gave an important history of another library,
Glasgow, and because it had also belonged at one time to the
Guildhall Library, which had passed it on to them.

In Oxford St Edmund Hall and New College had both made
large dispersals, and the shops were filled with books from their
stacks. I chose the St Edmund Hall book I did because it was by

a contemporary politician, and also because it was representative of one of the largest classes of dispersed books, those used by the immediately preceding generation: that is, those published in the fifties and sixties. The New College book was chosen because it was one that had been donated to the College by an author, a distinguished former Fellow of the College, no less than a Wykeham Professor, with others from his library for the use of future generations of scholars. There are several similar examples.

It is obvious that before the sample was obtained another form of natural selection had been in progress: earlier purchases by the public and by the booksellers themselves. When the Athenaeum Club disposed of its economics books the inscribed copies from the great Victorian economists were no doubt the first to find a new home. Generally the more expensive books would have gone already and only occasionally did I have to spend more than £5, often far less. This made things easier and established a genuine common base for the selection, for the commercial values of second-hand books are often the result of factors which are irrelevant when viewed in a scholarly perspective: that is, one which is concerned solely with the content of the book.

Two other factors are worth mentioning here because they are often given as reasons for dispersals that could not obviously be justified otherwise.

First, there is the question of condition: with a few exceptions the books listed have their entire life in front of them, certainly hundreds of years, and only a few are even what the booksellers would call 'reading copies'. They are by and large perfectly sound. The point is important, because conservation has recently become the subject of fierce debate. The central thesis is that from about 1850 onwards various experiments were made in paper production which changed drastically the estimated life of books. One can find examples of paper that has become so brittle that pages break away from their binding at a touch, and if anyone tries to handle the pages pieces break off. The projected preservation problem is great.

This is most common in America, and all the examples I have

seen have been in books printed there. It is difficult to find examples to correspond with the American experience in England. But this has not stopped some librarians latching on to the high cost of conservation as a reason for dispersing valuable books. David Vaisey, Bodley's Librarian in Oxford, remarked at the Loughborough seminar: 'There are dangers in using conservation as a kind of underhand means of directing a collecting strategy.' And indeed David Liddle, Director of Community Leisure in Avon, who is in charge of Avon County Libraries, seems to have taken this very line at the same seminar:

> Many libraries like ourselves have asked themselves to what extent the retention of these books [rare books] in any way contributes to the objectives of a modern public library. The answer is, of course, that they don't. A greater awareness amongst public librarians of the need to conserve rare books is quite likely to bring into sharper focus the whole question of whether the retention of those books is necessary, desirable or economic.[11]

The condition of the books in my list suggests that Vaisey is right and that, at least as far as English printed books are concerned, the justification of dispersal for reasons of 'preservation' is to be discounted.

The second factor is duplication. The British Library Act states quite clearly that books may be disposed of if they are duplicates, though this raises the question of what exactly a duplicate is. In some cases duplicates may not be bibliographically exactly the same. In fact none of the books in my list had any markings to suggest that they were duplicates; quite the reverse. One at least had on its title the small 'last copy' stamp. This system was used before the advent of on-line catalogues to ensure that at least one copy of a book remained in a library system, which was often county-wide and contained many branches. Clearly this system failed in the example here.

Early libraries

The easiest way to look at the wide variety of libraries in the list is to begin with the oldest. Since I acquired the books entirely at random some inevitably came from older libraries which had closed. I decided to keep them in the count because they gave an interesting sidelight on the history of lending libraries in England with some specific examples, and there were not too many of them.

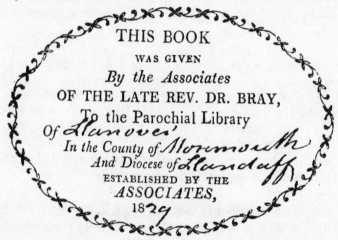

THIS BOOK WAS GIVEN By the Associates OF THE LATE REV. DR. BRAY, To the Parochial Library Of *Llanover* In the County of *Monmouth* And Diocese of *Llandaff* ESTABLISHED BY THE ASSOCIATES, 1829

The oldest book here is Kennett's *Roman Antiquities* published in 1699 and still in perfectly sound condition, though its plates have been removed by a 'breaker' – someone who removes all the maps and plates from a book, sells the plates, coloured and framed, to interior designers and other such people, and then throws the book away. Both the breaker and his designer customers are quintessential members of the semi-literate tendency. This particular book was one of many given to parochial libraries in England and America by the Associates of the Rev. Dr Bray (1656-1730) from 1709 onwards. In addition to hundreds of parish libraries in England endowed in this way there were over thirty founded by Dr Bray in America, the largest being in Annapolis. It may well be significant that the earliest subscription libraries were founded in America in the 1730s. The idea of Dr Bray's libraries or something very similar, but for the use of the lay public without any missionary purpose, spread across America backed by Benjamin Franklin and was soon re-exported to England, where it formed the basis of the public libraries as we know them, first as subscription libraries, then as public libraries supported by the rates.

Interestingly enough, another of Dr Bray's ideas concerned libraries at ports. Knowing that missionaries were liable to be stranded in such places for long periods, and that they were not without their temptations, he had the idea of setting up libraries there too as a wholesome diversion. Many survived through the centuries, and quite by chance there is here a book from the lineal descendant of one of them, the Sheerness Dockyard Library.

Two other early libraries listed, the Bredon Reading Society and the Lady Zetland reading circle, are interesting examples of a kind of library which seems now to have vanished entirely. It consisted of a small group of people whose names were printed in a list pasted on the endpapers of the volumes. As each reader received a book he put the date opposite his name, followed by the date on which he finished it, before sending it on to the next person on the list. There were 25 members of the Bredon Society and 20 in Lady Zetland's circle.

The next step up in size has some examples which are still going strong two centuries later. One in Devon has 70 members and is carried on much as when it was founded in 1799. It gets the papers and any books of local interest, and members have a key to let themselves in. The old simplicity of purpose and quiet efficiency continues as always, without any notice of the passing centuries; it has not been found necessary to install the telephone.

Many libraries on a slightly larger scale than this still survive and flourish outside the public library system. Those represented on the list here include the Devon and Exeter Institution, the Ipswich Institute, the Isle of Wight Institution – though in a modified form, it is still housed in its original listed building – and the Bath Royal Literary and Scientific Institution. This unfortunately is closed and boarded up, while its trustees,

Time allowed for reading, *21* days. Fine 6d. per week if kept beyond the time; and 1s. omitting to date.	DATE.	
	Received.	Past.
1 COUNTESS OF ZETLAND		
2 REV. JAMES WHARTON	*May 29*	*June 6*
3 MRS. GILPIN	*June 9*	*14*
4 ARCHDN. HEADLAM	*Feb 24*	*March 13*
5 MR. CLIFFORD	—	*Jany 18th*
6 MR. MORRITT	—	*Dec 19th*
7 REV. G. BOWNESS	*Nov 21*	*Dect 5*
8 MRS. WITHAM	*Jan 13*	*Feb 3*
9 REV. R. READE	*Feb 4th*	*Feb 24th*
10 MISS HUTCHINSON		
11 MR. HARTLEY		
12 MAJOR HEALEY	*Mar 13*	*March 29*
13 MRS. MORLEY	*March 25*	*April 9th*
14 REV. T. W. MORLEY	*July 17*	*May 4th*
Newfle Now 14.	*44*	*30 en*
15 REV. E. CUST	*July 19*	*Jul 26*
16 MRS. AYLMER	*August 13th*	*31th*
17 MR. WILSON	*July 11*	*August 13th*
18 REV. JOHN SWIRE	*Aug 30*	*Sep 13*
19 REV. W. G. SMITH	*Sept 13th*	*Nov 7*
20 REV. W. F. WHARTON	*Octr 10*	*Nov 14*

the Avon County Council, puzzle over its future and that of its important collections.

These libraries are now represented by the Association of Independent Libraries, made up entirely of Britain's surviving subscription libraries of which the most substantial is the London Library, this year celebrating its 150th anniversary. Some two million books are held in them and, with their stable specialised local collections, they are a valuable addition to the public system. The examples here, as will be seen, are books from their lending side, or books in need of repair. No doubt disposals of that kind will continue over the years, but in an organised way. They have weathered every kind of financial storm over the centuries and have skills which the public sector is only just beginning to learn. The only real threat to them is pressure to sell books that are particularly valuable, as happened to John Ryland's Library in Manchester a while ago, though that was not of course a private library. But even these pressures can usually be resisted nowadays.

Whether these libraries will become a model for the reform of a public library system which has become the plaything of politicians is another matter. Certainly those responsible for some of the decisions that have lead to outright closures could learn a lot by looking at these institutions which date back to the nineteenth century and earlier and will no doubt continue to survive.

These early subscription libraries, often in their listed buildings, were not the only ones used by the public. As the nineteenth century gathered pace many more libraries sprang up, as will be seen from examples given at the end of this book. There were countless small libraries that ran on into the 1930s and even later, right down to the small cornershop lending libraries of the kind George Orwell worked in (it is strange how, when you get down to the basic phenomena of literacy in England, he keeps cropping up). Orwell has left us with a graphic description of a typical reader, the elderly lady who always took out the same books, year-in year-out – a thing not possible incidentally in today's rapid-turnover public libraries – with the word, 'I *do* love a drop of Dell!' referring to the popular writer Ethel M. Dell. Miss Dell's books were still being re-printed for her admirers in the 1950s. Though this kind of book is now looked down on, it does represent a significant strand in popular literary culture, and is a world away from the glossy semi-literate illustrated books that seem more attractive.

Not all books borrowed from these libraries were of the Mills and Boon variety. An interesting example of a serious popular work unjustly neglected is seen here in the only book that occurs twice in the list: Morley Roberts's *The Colossus*. Its survival from two small circulating libraries shows its contemporary popularity, and the issue stamps still present in one of them show that it was out continuously for years. Anyone trying seriously to find out what was in the public mind at the time of the Boer War and the years leading up to the First World War will find information here of great value. Indeed by the standards of modern fiction it is eminently worth reprinting. The likelihood of finding it on a University reading list, or even in a University library, would be slight, though the books of Roberts's lifelong friend George Gissing do have a place in the approved literary canon.

While many of these libraries were on this small scale there were giants also. Smith's ran lending libraries, as has already been mentioned, but the real giant of the Victorian age was Mudie's. Books with their yellow Mudie's label still appear in large numbers, and their contribution to the literary culture of the time must have been high indeed. At first the public lending libraries did not compete with Mudie's and their kin. Some refused to have fiction on their shelves at all. Others, such as Ealing Public Library, made a formal arrangement to carry Mudie's books and act as agent for them. This serious quality in the public libraries survived into the interwar years. They were known, with truth, as 'The People's Universities'. But at some point they decided to compete with the lending libraries in their own field. The results were not to be entirely bad, as we shall see in the next section. But the results for the private lending libraries were catastrophic. Mudie's went early on. The Boots Booklovers Library, the nearest modern equivalent, survived until the sixties; the branch in Exeter closed in 1965. By that time the public library had changed its character completely. It had taken on the private circulating libraries and won, but in winning the battle it lost a war, perhaps even the war that Gladstone so acutely saw they were fighting. It is a tribute to the Boots system that they are still by far the most common ex-library books. Often, when some rare modern book is looked for, it is a Boots copy that is finally located. Its only rival is the *Times* lending library.

The public libraries

Richard Hoggart, author of a much admired post-war book, *The Uses of Literacy*, remarked recently:

> The tide flows strongly in favour of the populist, the valueless public library...the Library service has lost its soul and, desperately seeking some justification for its existence, veers between pop-marketing in imitation of the big chains – the McDonald's and Burger Kings of the printed word – and trying to be a sub-branch of information processing.[12]

The public library has lost its soul because it has been absorbed into the modern semi-literate culture and because it did not have the knowledge and experience gained across generations that the old private libraries had to enable them to cope with the world of mass circulation popular fiction, for example, rather than the People's University that Hoggart remembers from his youth in the Hunslet district of Leeds.

Because the old private lending libraries were commercial organisations they became adept at managing their stock. On the question of disposals they all developed considerable skills. Books from Boots Library had small labels in them which, if a reader wanted to buy it when it had finished its circulation life, he could fill in and give to the librarian when he returned it. This had been a practice for many years, as the label from Day's circulating library illustrated overleaf shows. Harrods Library, which had an extensive clientele, used to publish long lists of ex-library books which could be bought at a third of the price when new, or less if rebound for library use. All these systems

DAY'S LIBRARY, Ltd.,

FOUNDED 1776.   **96, MOUNT STREET, LONDON, W.**

For EARLY SECOND-HAND *Copies of this work*, SUB-
SCRIBERS AND OTHERS *wishing to purchase the same are
respectfully requested to send their names to the Librarian, who
will send particulars of price as soon as the first demand for
the book has abated.*

Scarce Books and Books out of print carefully searched for.

*A List of Surplus Books is published Monthly, and may
be had regularly on application.*

dealt with the problem of how to dispose of stock when, as Day's
library so elegantly put it on the slip, 'the first demand for the
book has abated'. Even this basic level of skill has still to be
mastered by the average public library. And the method they
have adopted has proved to be the beginning of the slide that
has lead to mass dispersals of the kind that happened at Brent.

For a long time dispersal of any book from a public library
was considered anathema. This desirable attitude dated from
the days of the Victorian foundation of the system when
dispersal of books which had been bought with ratepayers'
money would have seemed like culpable negligence. The
decision to compete with the fiction lending libraries altered
things, but for a while the old remedy of pulping was resorted
to, sometimes with amusing consequences as the flood of
popular titles reached ever greater strength. The novelist Jack
Trevor Story describes how he was once seeking a copy of an
early book of his, *The Trouble with Harry*. All his efforts had
failed when one day he saw a copy in his local library in a
container of discarded books. He explained his predicament to
the librarian but was told that the book was due to be pulped
and it did not matter that he was the author. Nothing he could
do or say would move this stalwart protector of civic rectitude
from his ordained path. The book was pulped.

Sept.-Oct. 1929.   Sale List No. 87.

LIBRARY
BOOKS

AT

50% to 80%

Below the Original Prices.

The Librarian invites an inspection of the stock of works of History, Biography ⁓ ⁓ ⁓ and Fiction, that are not included in ⁓ ⁓ ⁓. his stock chiefly consists of books ⁓ ⁓ ⁓ is available.

*Order from*_____

_____

_____

Harrods Circulating Library

Harrods Ltd Knightsbridge London S W 1

OUT OF PRINT BOOKS
SEARCHED FOR FREE OF CHARGE.

Today this surely could not happen. The book would have been sold from the row of shelves to be found in every public library for the price of a daily paper. This system is better than the absolute waste of pulping, but it leads to major breakdowns of a kind that the private libraries would not have allowed under any circumstances. Besides the semi-literate glossies, and the best-selling 'page-turners' that have to be moved aside for the next over-hyped wave, books appear for sale that are of a quite different kind.

The libraries that Hoggart remembers as giving him his first education in English literature acquired serious books of every kind. The distinguished chemist Lord Dainton described recently how the finding of a book on valency at his public library in Sheffield had been a seminal experience in his life. It started him out on a career which must have been exactly the kind envisaged by Gladstone and the pioneers of the public library system. Lord Dainton wondered whether the Sheffield library authorities would have purchased an equivalent book today. No doubt he had in mind Sheffield's recently announced decision to stop all book purchases as a response to the 'cuts'. To which we might add the question whether the book he read is still there.

It does not need great intelligence or 'professionalism' to realise that the dispersal of *those* kinds of books is not the same thing as clearing popular fiction. But, as we shall see in a minute, that was exactly what was happening. It is not clear whether the transition from one quite understandable activity to another that would have made the old commercial librarians blush even to contemplate (one thinks of Day's library ticket with its 'Scarce books and books out of print carefully searched for') was simply a question of the slippery slope in a semi-literate world. A half-understood commercialism seems to have permeated the library schools where readers are referred to as 'customers'. Armed with this perspective, library staff may perhaps be more likely to respond to the specious logic of their political masters, eager to turn an honest penny as long as it will cause controversy *and* save money from the Westminster rate-cappers.

It is dispersals of this People's University of books bequeathed by the Victorians and their successors up to the

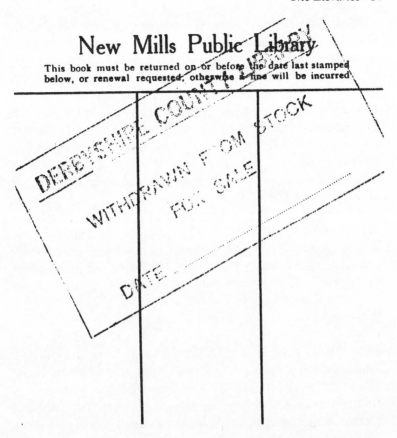

postwar years that are the real reason for the library's losing its soul, as Richard Hoggart so aptly put it. I discovered a classic example during my research: the Mackie Memorial Library donated in 1895 to the New Mills Technical Institute. The labels in the book chart its passage from the Memorial Library to the Technical Institute, thence to the New Mills Public Library and finally, at some unspecified date, out into the wide world when the collection was dispersed by Derbyshire County Council.

At the very time this highly specialised library of books on the cotton industry was being dispersed, without even being checked against the holdings of the British Library – the book here listed is not to be found in their catalogue – the New Mills

Heritage Centre was trying to put together a collection of books which would be of use to students visiting what had been, among other achievements, the home of the British calico printing industry. The Mackie Memorial Library had been put together for just this purpose a hundred years before, and these were the very books being sold by Derbyshire library staff. When the facts became known through contact established with the Curator of the New Mills Heritage Centre, some action was taken and all Mackie Memorial Library books that could be found in local bookshops were bought back by the Derbyshire authorities. But the damage had been largely done.

The poignancy of this catastrophe is the greater when it is realised that Andrew Carnegie, the greatest benefactor the British public library system has ever known, was himself a cotton man who started life as a boy in a cotton mill. The New Mills public library from which the Mackie collection was discarded was paid for by Carnegie.

Brent

Perhaps the most serious dispersal of this kind was from Brent Library in the mid-1980s. The facts came to light when a former Brent librarian, J.T. Gillet, read the good news that a new library had been opened in Brent. Something struck him as odd about the number of books cited for the new library. When he checked, the number that had 'gone missing' was found to be in six figures. He wrote a letter to the *Library Association Record* asking a few basic questions:

> It cannot be easy to explain away the disappearance of 105,070 books from the stock of Brent Central Library at Willesden Green as part of the £8 million scheme of development. I affirm it to have been a fine active stock of books which ought to be available in any good library service...Books issued from the library over the year (1968) totalled 428,712, of which 142,723 were non-fiction so it could by no means be regarded as dead stock.[13]

There was a loud silence from the authorities in Brent. Eventually a letter appeared which must be one of the most damaging library letters ever published, as well as being deeply moving:

A sorry tale of missing books

'Where have all Brent's books gone?' asks J.T. Gillett (August *Record*). In lieu of an official response I shall be pleased to enlighten him. Between 1980 and 1985 I was a librarian in Brent's Bibliographic Department, and thus reasonably close to the centre of things in matters of stock. Although I am not in a position to provide any of the detailed statistics Mr Gillett calls for, I can certainly tell the sad tale of the missing books.

As I think Mr Gillett already suspects, the truth is that a great part of the Willesden Green library stock was sacrificed on the altar of Community Librarianship. This trend began around 1979, when the then library management team enthusiastically embraced the recommendations of the Hillingdon Report...

At the same time, the left-wing sympathies of Brent Council allowed the inverted nazism of Radical Librarianship free rein to withdraw (i.e. censor) anything that offended its sensibilities. Consequently there was a witch-hunt for any books that could possibly be construed as sexist, racist, colonialist, etc, which were fallen upon with all the fury of a Puritan iconoclast. The depredations of this form of Macarthyism/Librarianship were severe, although not as bad as at another library in the borough where the Greenhamism of the librarian in charge compelled her to withdraw all books on the subject of war. Many other worthwhile books were, like them, consigned to pulp or book sales because they were simply 'irrelevant to the community', so as to make room for the multiple copies of paperbacks from Pluto Press and the like which the community apparently needed more.

Less blameworthy, but ultimately perhaps more tragic, was the fate of an older and larger reserve collection, housed nearby in an old warehouse. This had to be demolished to make way for the new library complex and it was impossible to find alternative accommodation for all the books stored there. A small group of professionals, myself included, selected those books which we believed should be saved at all costs but, although we did this as conscientiously as possible, our combined subject knowledge was at best partial and it is inevitable that some books worthy of preservation were overlooked ... Finally, there was no other course left but a mammoth book sale at the annual Brent Show, where several thousand books were disposed of at an average price of about 50p each. Several thousand others left unsold were pulped...

Alan M. Linfield
Tring, Herts[14]

Subsequent correspondence established that the facts in the letter were correct. The defence given by some of those who had authorised this unparalleled act of iconoclasm in modern England, while clearly sincere, points to the narrow perspectives that had allowed the events to occur. The spirit of the answers is seen in this extract from one of the letters:

Whatever the image of Brent, now and in the past, I would applaud it, in my time there, for honestly addressing issues of selection policy that most other authorities were too faint-hearted to address [the *ad hominem* attack is typical]. They were matters of concern to people in Brent then, and probably now, of racism and sexism. In contradiction to Mr Linfield's opinion as expressed in his letter, I believe the policies set in place resulted in procedures that all librarians now, working in multi-cultural communities, would consider quite reasonable and normal. Thank goodness for pioneers.[15]

If ruthlessly destroying a hundred years of tradition, not to mention a massive loss of capital, is 'pioneering', then it must surely rank with the pioneering attempts of Stalin in purging Soviet libraries of all books that departed from his orthodoxy. The Nazis also pioneered in the field of book destruction in their self-imposed task of reducing the multi-cultural nature of German society by the elimination of that quintessentially literate people whom Stalin referred to as 'cosmopolitan elements'. One wonders if there were any books by Jewish authors in the 105,070 that went in Brent. No doubt there were. In which case those who perpetrated this outrage on British culture are in good company, whether they were flying the flag of 'racism and sexism' or not.

*

Another element in the break-up of libraries is the advent of computers. The connection between computers and library dissolution is surprisingly direct, as two brief examples make clear. A librarian at Westminster, who took an extremely responsible attitude to dispersals, remarked in the course of an article:

> When in 1982 it was decided that all lending records should be computerised, wholesale book withdrawals took place in order to rationalise the stock throughout the Westminster system.[16]

But sometimes there was a more direct connection, as David Liddle of Avon County Council described in a contribution to the seminar referred to earlier:

> We recently had to face this problem in my own county when we embarked on a capital programme to computerise the library service. We had somewhere to find annual running costs of about £100,000 a year out of the existing budget. We did two things to offset this: first of course we reduced the book fund [the money for purchase of new books]. The second thing we did was to sell off some of the rare books in order to provide capital which we could apply to the capital cost of the computer system. We were not the first and I am sure we will not be the last to respond to financial pressures by selling off rare books. These are the books which it is nice to have which cost a lot to look after, but which nobody can actually ever look at because they are so valuable.[17]

It is an irony that underlying this kind of dispersal policy, which can of course be criticised, is a reliance on the old skills that the private librarians would have had at their finger tips. These are now to be found only in the book sale-rooms, the most important of which are Bloomsbury Book Auctions in London and Dominic Winter Book Auctions of Swindon, and among antiquarian dealers. These people supply the expert knowledge which is lacking, and save the librarian embarrassment by acting as a shield between the disposing library and the purchaser. The purchaser, more often than not, is a University or institutional library which has *not* forgotten the value of books that previous generations have preserved – in this case for the people of England, though the libraries that end up owning the books are usually abroad.

A further irony, especially in provincial centres, is that the reliance upon the book 'trade' is often combined with an amused disdain:

> Selling to the antiquarian and second-hand book trade is more lucrative...It has been quite an eye-opener for us. A selection of pre-1700 books fetched two and a half times its valuation; a sale of duplicate art portfolios and fine printing had the 'big boys' from London falling over each other...New pastures indeed and I regret my lack of education in historical bibliography.[18]

At times, as I have researched this book, it has occurred to me that the second-hand book world is the only place left in England where knowledge of anything but the latest semi-literate fads still exists. But this of course is an exaggeration; it exists in the still-literate public – the customers, used in its correct sense, of the booksellers, and those who are in a real sense custodians of England's literary culture, the staff and students of the Universities and large copyright libraries. Perhaps the most serious worry is that these institutions too are disposing of books. And their traditions go back much further than the mid-Victorian aspirations embodied in the Public Library Acts.

Educational libraries

A glance at the list of institutions discarding books will show that the largest single category is teacher-training colleges, which have been subjected to more than their fair share of amalgamations and closures in recent years. The following changes have occurred among those listed:

Balls Park College, later Hertfordshire College of Higher Education, is now Hatfield Polytechnic (Wall Hall Campus).
Brighton Training College is now Brighton Polytechnic.
Elizabeth Gaskell College of Education and City of Manchester College of Higher Education are both now Manchester Polytechnic.
The College of St Mathias Bristol is now Bristol Polytechnic.
Neville's Cross College is now New College Durham.
The College of Education Ripon is now the College of Ripon and York St John.
St Luke's College Exeter is now Exeter University.
South Downs College no longer exists.[19]

And more could be added. The effect of these amalgamations, as far as this survey is concerned, has been to put onto the market what must be a large proportion of the original libraries. There were far more teacher-training college libraries than any other kind of library from which multiple examples appeared in the shops. In one bookshop in Kent you might have imagined for a moment that you were actually *in* a teacher-training college library. Almost every book taken down was from the same college.

The exact logic behind these dispersals remains obscure. Unfortunately, though it is an area of greatest interest, it is also one most difficult to get information about. Because of the many controversies within the educational system, and the strong teacher organisations, those responsible are extremely reluctant to comment at all. At one point I made a straightforward attempt to discover what principles were followed in the amalgamation of libraries which clearly would have involved duplication and manifold reasons for legitimate dispersals. I made an appointment with the head librarian of a prominent teacher-training college. Within a few hours he cancelled it on the grounds that the subject was 'too sensitive' – some twelve years after the amalgamation of his library had taken place. He explained to me that the interview had been cancelled on the order of his superiors – and he was himself the head librarian!

The reader will have to judge the scale and significance of the disposals for himself. He may perhaps speculate with me on whether the widely reported drop in standards of literacy among children of school-leaving age can in any way be connected with the massive dispersals and changes which have taken place in these educational libraries. It is clear that the proximate cause has been government action. This time it is not a matter of rate-capping and 'the cuts', though they no doubt played a part, but of decisions to recast teacher training. The extreme difficulty in getting information suggests some state secret. In America, with its Freedom of Information Act (long overdue here), such secrecy could not occur. After all, it is everyone's children who stand to suffer from theories which, to take only one example, disdain the teaching of history in factual terms.

Military and other libraries

There are libraries which have a legitimate reason for being subject to the Official Secrets Act, and a number of them are represented here. They are the armed forces libraries. Clearly these libraries might contain information that would be of use to an enemy. None the less there has been a quite open policy of dispersal as cutbacks have led to the closing of bases at home

and abroad. The wide range and quality of these libraries is obvious. From society's point of view the only question is whether those who had the benefit of these excellent libraries in the forces will have the same access to books when they leave. If not, there will have been a real loss, which will no doubt add to the rising tide of semi-literacy.

The tradition of literacy in the army goes back to the seventeenth century and the Civil War, which was fought with texts and pamphlets as much as with weapons, and beyond to the Reformation, and beyond that again to the mediaeval orders of chivalry such as the Knights Templar. The church militant, and indeed all ecclesiastical and monastic institutions, possessed libraries and were repositories of learning. The dissolution of the monasteries in Henry VIII's reign has never been forgotten. The fate of the monastic libraries serves in popular imagination as a classic example of mindless iconoclasm. At least one bookseller remarked to me that so many ex-library books had come on to the market in the last few years that he had begun to realise what it must have been like when the great monastic libraries were being dispersed. And if his comparison was contrived, it is no less valid for that.

The comparison is a literal one as far as the abbeys and other religious houses in the list of libraries here are concerned. Today the reasons for dispersal are of course internal, apart from the general rise in costs, and are similar to those given for dispersals in private institutional lending libraries. Reduced congregations exactly parallel reduced readership. However, both have weathered storms before and are used to surviving in adverse times. Indeed when times get bad things are often better for them as people turn back to the old faiths. It is interesting that holdings of libraries of the Established Church are rarely seen. Only a handful are to be found in this collection. No doubt, as they are established, the pressures for dispersal are fewer. Only the occasional public scandal, such as the attempt to sell the *Mappa Mundi* at Hereford Cathedral, disturbs the calm. And here again the temptation was one that has been noted before as an ever-present danger to the private lending libraries: the pressure to sell off a single very valuable asset.

University libraries

The only mediaeval institutions to survive through to the present day are of course the older Universities. It is true they did not survive unscathed and that the Bodleian Library was founded well after the Reformation, but many a manuscript discarded from the monasteries fetched up in the possession of one of the colleges, and private men such as Sir Thomas Bodley soon repaired the broken links.

Sadly, as can be seen from the list of dispersals, even the older colleges have found it necessary to dispose of books. Unlike the dispersals of the teacher-training college libraries, which are surrounded by an emotional and controversial aura, those from the older Universities are frequently discussed and the causes and problems are widely realised. What is not readily to hand is a valid general assessment of the damage which the disposals may be doing. There have also been occasional errors of judgment, regretted by all but recognised to have been caused by the harsh financial climate on the one hand and the immense flood of new books demanding funds and shelving on the other.

An interesting perspective on the nature of the problem can be given by a graph plotting the number of dispersals against the date of publication of the books disposed of. The overwhelming bulk will be seen to be the fifties and sixties. Since the sample taken was entirely random and 292 is a statistically significant proportion of the total number of libraries, it may be possible to make a hypothesis on the basis of this graph.

What seems to have occurred is that the texts of the previous generation have been disposed of in preference to any others. Teachers constructing lists for students no doubt remember these books from their youth and are therefore more conscious of their failings and believe them to have been superseded by their own books and those of their colleagues. But if these kinds of books are discarded the dialogue between the generations vanishes. The historical development which can be found in any long-established library also goes. A Thatcherite economist may despise the Keynesian clap-trap praised, indeed worshipped, by previous generations of lecturers, but if he strips the library of all Keynesian texts his students will undoubtedly lose perspective.

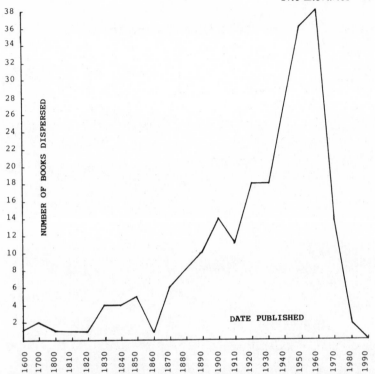

These are of course generalisations. In teacher-training colleges lecturers have new theories of history that do away with the learning of 'facts' in favour of imaginative ident- ification with characters whose personalities are presented to pupils with more than a little colouring from the modern stereotypes that possess their own imagination. They are un- likely to be worried if 'boring old history books' are discarded. Using historical continuity as an argument for keeping twenty- and thirty-year- old text books would be thought absurd. Such arguments would not hold sway in a University, let alone in an Oxbridge College, but economic pressures may force their librarians along a path beaten by professional colleagues in another part of the wood.

The question that people who are forced to decide whether to discard or not are liable to ask is: 'What have the students actually lost if these books go? We will, after all, be gaining space and making a few bob.' To which the obvious reply is another question: 'Where else could they read these books?' Here again, despite the relatively small sample, we can answer the question by looking at other libraries. The obvious place to go is the British Library. All but four of the books in the list can be found in its catalogue, a good average for a small sample. But the next step is to look at the catalogue of a good University library. Here the percentage drops sharply. I found only 35 per cent of the books in the catalogue of the nearest library of this standard. Even excluding the admittedly 'popular' works included in what is a random list, many of the volumes I did not find were by authors who were represented by other titles. Some of the missing texts were significant. The real loss would appear to be substantial. What is one institution's discard is another's desideratum.

Since most university students work from books to hand and find it impracticable to wait for inter-library loan requests – and you cannot browse an inter-library loan book before it arrives, any more than you can browse the contents of books in the memory of an 'on-line' catalogue and not on a shelf in front of you – the result is a major diminution of standards. The situation in Oxbridge and London is clearly less serious, since there the copyright libraries are to hand. But for too long the cry of librarians disposing of books willy-nilly has been: 'You worry too much. There's always the BL (or the Bod, or wherever).' The feelings of the copyright libraries when they hear these words is best summed up by Bodley's Librarian himself:

> The sort of 'asset-stripping' advocated by David Liddle is neither desirable nor possible for me. Mine is one of those libraries which picks up the tab...[20]

Unfortunately the single-copy fallacy, the idea that it is enough that there should be one copy of any book in existence, does have support even within the British Library itself. Lord Quinton remarked at the Loughborough seminar:

> All we can do is to try and insure against the possibility of ill-judged disposal by some sort of division of labour. It would take the form of a general application of the

principle generally applied by national libraries, that of preserving the total literary output of the nation in question. So long as there is one copy somewhere modern techniques of microphotography can make the text widely and rapidly available if there is a demand for it.[21]

While the idea of preserving the total literary output of a nation is the ideal to be aimed at – an ideal relied upon by those who discard gleefully – the fact is that the British Library does *not* have a copy of every book. Anyone who has done serious research will realise this immediately. Our brief list contains four which are not to be found in the BL catalogue as we have seen. There are indeed whole areas in which the British Library has patchy holdings. One is of particular interest for anyone studying the evolution of dust-jacket design, a key aspect of the rise of semi-literacy this century.

For many years the British Library has not acquired copies of books which are simply reprints of what they already have: that is, later editions identical in text and pagination with first editions of books popular enough to be reprinted. This means that the dust-jackets of later editions, which relied more and more on their design to ensure sale to a mass audience, are not to be found there. Anyone wishing to study the phenomenon will have to go elsewhere.

It could be argued that this is of little moment, as only popular texts are involved. But owing to the rise of semi-literacy 'serious' hardback novels, and indeed books in general, are nowadays bought on impulse on the design of the jacket alone. A narcissistic concern with visual appearance accords with the best efforts of sales and marketing teams, and the design of any book is a vital factor. Today almost anything goes as long as the right jacket is there to gull the public. Books which, in pre-jacket days, would not have passed any reader are now accepted as long as the 'presentation' is right. Many retailers today rely simply on jacket design and advertising budgets and never bother to read a text at all. It is perhaps as well that the British Library does not concern itself with such phenomena, but the absence of the raw material means, again, that it cannot be studied properly at what is the centre of literary culture *par excellence.*

There are more serious types of books which are often absent from the British Library. One is the modern political pamphlet. To cite a small example from my own research, anyone wishing to examine, say, the strange attempt at a revolution in Britain in January 1941 that went by the name of 'The People's Convention' will have difficulty in the British Library. Only a handful of the numerous pamphlets that were published at the time are included in the catalogue. Even the Convention manifesto is not listed. The single-copy fallacy operates here strongly, for the only way to study the Convention is through copies in the 'real world': that is copies obtained at the time and held since by those who attended or their heirs. I had to rely on such copies. For any text to live it must be available in the community from which it sprang. It is for this reason that totalitarian governments, and even quasi-totalitarian governments, employ censorship. To say that one copy is sufficient and that it is probably available at the British Library is good enough grounds for an organisation such as Brent Library to throw out books that are ideologicaly unsound, as unquestionably it did.

When faced with such happenings as those at Brent, and the perceived attitudes of *avant garde* librarians that the BL is the answer for every query for books beyond the current hit-list, the British Library does, clearly, have a vital role to play. It is the last bastion against all these evils, and will remain so as long as it keeps acquiring books it does not have when they are found and brought to it. But there is a nagging doubt that the British Library itself will fall prey to the semi-literate tendency – it is after all located in Bloomsbury itself. There are a number of books in the list here that have been discarded from the British Library, including an *editio princeps*. But developments in the eighties suggest that these fears are not as worrying as the very real fear about other libraries in Britain.

As long ago as the seventeenth century worries have been expressed about the inadequacies of official libraries. Richard Bentley, the great classical scholar, Master of Trinity College, Cambridge, who was appointed Keeper of the King's Libraries in 1694, answered criticism in terms that could be used today:

> I will own that I have often said and lamented that the library was not fit to be seen...If the room be too mean, and too little for the books; if it be too much out of repair; if the situation be inconvenient; if the access to it be dishonourable; is the library keeper to answer for it? ...The expenses and toils of a long war are but too just an excuse that the thought of a new library were not part of the public cares.[22]

The modern equivalent of the long war is the burden of the armaments race and the un-English bureaucracy, legacy of two world wars, that still stifles the country despite a decade of Mrs Thatcher's administration. However, thanks to the efforts of Lord Dainton, and his rapport with Mrs Thatcher, whose tutor he was at Oxford, we are to get the New Library that in Bentley's day could not be thought of, though the Victorians created an ideal solution for their day. Mrs Thatcher's decision to back the library despite economic setbacks surely outweighs the decision to disperse the Conservative Party's own research library. It is only to be hoped that dispersals of any kind are restricted on the most severe criteria, and that money for acquisitions, storage and, perhaps most important, staff for cataloguing is not stinted. Immense sums are being spent on the storage of nuclear waste.

Storage of the country's literary heritage is at least as important, and neglect of this heritage by dispersal will be just as damaging.

4

The Rise of Semi-Literacy

Throughout this short book it has been suggested that the rise of semi-literacy and the dispersal of libraries are inter-related phenomena, the one feeding off the other to create a climate in which books and their contents become less and less important. And one of the prime factors most often pointed to as a cause has been the rise of the new media of communication and entertainment, particular emphasis being placed on the deleterious effects of television. The books here have been collected entirely at random, as has been explained, but it is interesting to see that the arrival of the new media is reflected in some of them quite significantly. To use the analogy of the archaeological site once more, there are finds which can tell us a great deal. The first group concerns radio.

Radio

Unlike television, radio had an effect on literacy that was almost entirely positive. There sprang into existence a new kind of book of which Cyril Burt's *How the Mind Works* is a good example, despite the cloud under which some of his own work has recently fallen. The text of the book is made up of the scripts of programmes broadcast in a radio series and then edited and developed. When these series were put out over the air the BBC, then a monopoly, published pamphlets to accompany them. Listening circles were set up which bear a strong resemblance to those used for today's Open University programmes.

Many were published in *The Listener* and later in book form. Those who heard the programmes read the book and a vast new audience was reached.

A new branch of literature developed just for radio. Muriel Spark's book listed here, *Voices at Play*, is based on material written solely for the medium. Una Marson's poems and some of her contributions to the wartime broadcast poetry magazine *Voice* have recently been reprinted.

Radio produced a new kind of political commentator, far removed from the hidebound political columnist of the newspapers, epitomised by the American Fred Kaltenborn. He gave events a new reality for those who had hardly realised that politicians were people just like themselves – presumably the Karl Marx Memorial Library acquired the copy here on the principle 'Know thine Enemy'. It was discarded when shelving had to be cleared away from a wall on which a mural had been discovered after being painted over in the Stalinist era when the artist who created it had fallen out of favour.

The dark side of radio politics cannot be better illustrated than by Sefton Delmer's *Black Boomerang*, an account of the murky world of Britain's black radio propaganda put out during the war. The copy here came, appropriately enough, from the public library at Brentford, scene of John Wilkes's great electoral triumphs at the Middlesex hustings in the 1760s, not a stone's throw from the library, on the area of ground, still public land, known as The Butts. The library itself is yet another of Carnegie's donations and, like the Carnegie Library at New Mills, it has also lost its original collection of books on Brentford acquired at great cost and expense over many years. It is now a basic lending library.

Television

Television is different. Though there is a case to be made for its use as an educational medium – and the BBC's contribution to the Open University at Milton Keynes has been considerable, if politically questionable, and will continue despite the closure of their studios in a fine example of accountant's false logic –

this has not been the main area of impact. A text listed here from America in 1960 provides an indication of the possibilities seen for educational television at its most hopeful phase. It has not fulfilled those hopes except in certain 'closed circuit' situations, where the viewers are very restricted in number, or others where the main channels are used but at unsocial hours. In reality what American television has become for most people around the world is an endless series of detective programmes, game shows, chat shows and soaps of every variety.

Though the hoped-for explosion of educational television has not happened the effect has not been entirely negative as far as literacy goes. 'Tie-in books' are a major part of any best-seller list, but not all of them are of the semi-literate kind often found there and described earlier. The downside, as far as concerns book publishing in general, is that the lower-grade extended-caption tie-ins hog the limelight and drive out 'real' books which might otherwise be given more shelf space, and which would almost certainly be of far greater merit in themselves. The close link in Britain between television series and the best-seller lists is not reflected worldwide. And the peculiarly British nature of the phenomenon is emphasised by the fact that it is almost always BBC tie-in books that are involved. This is due not to their merit, but to the extensive free advertising they have benefited from which is not available to their competitors.

The BBC's vigorous prosecution of its commercial ends in this way is in stark contrast to such acts as the closing of *The Listener*, the selling off of irreplaceable books from its library and the closing of the Open University studios. These three decisions alone show the cutting-edge of semi-literacy winning over the high cultural standards that the BBC is supposed to stand for, and indeed the justification – the only one – for the subvention of over a billion pounds a year from the British tax-payer. However, despite the best efforts of the BBC and other giant mass publishing houses to clog the best-seller lists with the epitome of semi-literate publishing, literacy keeps breaking through in the most unlikely places, and nearly always from American rather than British programmes. The television series

Twin Peaks produced a rash of books that will be read in true page-turner style by legions of devotees. Further they are in recognised literary genres, such as the diary – *The Diary of Laura Palmer*, for example – and, apart from the obligatory cover photograph, are filled with words from cover to cover.

Cinema

By the same token the cinema industry in America, which has dominated the twentieth century and contributed more than any other force to the primacy of the visual image, does also create new audiences for books which are sold as 'the book of the film' despite their having been in print as classics for many years. They can also create audiences for books which before had only a slight following, and sometimes the making of a film leads to success for the author of the book on which the film was based simply as an author.

The publicity for *The Silence of the Lambs* produced not only a successful 'book of the film' by Thomas Harris, but a success for an earlier book of his which, although filmed, had not had any impact at the box-office. This is clearly a literary phenomenon, or rather an example of literacy at work in place of the semi-literacy that might naively be associated with the film industry; people who had read one book by the author then sought out his earlier book, putting it too on the best-seller list.

Again, while these books are in the 'horror' genre which the twentieth century has made its own, they are not written without an eye to their context in literary history beyond their descent from Mary Shelley's *Frankenstein* and the Gothic novel. *The Silence of the Lambs* has epigraphs from Donne's *Devotions* and the First Book of Corinthians and other allusions which will ensure its place on reading lists, at least in America. The newly risen semi-literacy in England means that it is likely that those who read the book after seeing the film will not be able to find the works of Donne and other classic authors alluded to in the book in their local libraries. They will have been 'dumped' along with the other books by 'yesterday's men and women'. Perhaps some courageous reader will insist that the books are ordered,

and the tide of semi-literacy will have been held back to that
extent through the unsuspected influence of the popular
cinema.

Videos

Nor is the video industry, which has sprung into life in barely a
decade, necessarily a sign of semi-literacy. In a strange way the
appearance of video libraries in almost every imaginable retail
outlet exactly parallels the development of the lending library
in Victorian times. They give us a vivid idea of what the lending
libraries would be like if the popular mass-circulation libraries
had not been crushed by the public libraries in their politically
motivated post-war form. The selling of book tie-ins in video
outlets cannot be far behind. Perhaps the accidental resemblance of a video in its box to a book in its dust-jacket will lead
a child to pick up a book by mistake, thinking it to be a video,
and start reading. Hope springs eternal! And perhaps the greatest value of the video has been to reduce the time the average
family spends watching the effluvia of television served up on
the two main British television channels whose only role in the
future looks more and more likely to be news and sport. Oh yes
– and politics.

Politics

Since the rise of semi-literate England as seen in the dissolution
of so many libraries is something that only political action will
be able to solve – in an age when, despite a decade of 'Thatcher-
ism' and a supposed return to Victorian standards, the state is
still all-powerful – it is suitable to end on a political note. Those
who have the job of seeing that political studies libraries are kept
up may well ask themselves if there is any point. Surely all that
is needed are those volumes of *Yes, Minister* and the works of
Dobbs and Archer, together with a beginner's guide to political
advertising. Who needs political literacy? And if Central Office
have dumped their library why shouldn't we? Semi-literacy
reigns!

There is more than a grain of truth in this scenario, despite Mrs Thatcher's undoubted role in the creation of the new British Library building. In a semi-literate age politicians are fragile; they live by and through institutions which were developed at a time when speech-writers were unknown and MPs were elected on policies evolved without feedback, positive or negative, from market researchers. The people do not *know* what has changed, but they sense that something has. Many date Mrs Thatcher's real loss of credibility with the public to her own appearance on *Yes, Minister*; fanciful perhaps, but in a semi-literate age who can tell what apparently innocent excursion will not produce serious results? The magic of the media, their glamour, means that anything can happen.

In the middle of the worst recession since the war we now have a new crop of party political broadcasts, and a fresh set of posters, both crafted with skill by the advertising industry's finest, which have had an immediate effect. This is the reality of politics in an age of semi-literate dialogue combined with cynical market-research-led *Realpolitik*.

It is perhaps hardly surprising then that, faced with this kind of system in operation, councillors in Derbyshire and elsewhere should fight back with their own *Realpolitik* and hit where they think the effect will be most controversial. But with bitter consequences, for the target they have chosen is the very thing they should be preserving at all costs.

The books in the list were, with few exceptions, selected by the random methods explained. They were chosen simply because they were from a library and had been cast out. They are the closest thing to a random selection of books printed in English that anyone might find in any shop, a fair sample of our literature which just happens to have been discarded as worthless. Does it matter? As far as the politicians and those in public service standing behind them are concerned, it seems that they really couldn't care less. The strange rise of semi-literate England? They are proud to be part of it. Even proud to be the cause.

Sample List of Institutions

The numbers which follow each library on this list refer to the
books themselves in the list that follows.

1. Admiralty Library **149**
2. Albert Park Rowing Club Library **131**
3. Army Christian Leadership Training Centre MELF **172**
4. Armstrong College, Newcastle-upon-Tyne **195**
5. Army School of Education, Beaconsfield **91**
6. Ashridge Library **173**
7. Athenaeum Library **34**
8. Author's Club **35**
9. Avon County Library **133**

10. Ayr Carnegie Library **79**
11. Balls Park College Library **94**
12. Bank of England Library and Literary Association **106**
13. Barking Public Library **206**
14. Barnet Public Library **114**

15. Bath Municipal Library **234**
16. Bath Royal Literary Institution and Reading Society **84**
17. Belleisle Servants Library **230**
18. Bibliotheca Congr. SS Redempt. Domus B.M.V. Immaculatae de Victoriis, Clapham **165**
19. Birmingham Assay Office Staff Library **170**
20. Bishopsgate Institute, London **76**
21. Bredon Book Society **221**
22. Bodmin, Canonicorum Regularium Lateranensium **37**
23. Boots Booklovers Lending Library **18; 168**
24. Bourneville Works Library **147**
25. Brentford and Chiswick Public Libraries **71**
26. Brighton Polytechnic **49**
27. Brighton Training College **49**
28. Bristol Public Libraries **27**
29. British Broadcasting Corporation Library **167**
30. British Chapel at Rome Lending Library **198**
31. British Electricity Authority Southern Division Technical Library **19**
32. British Library Boston Spa **254**
33. British Library Central Library **139**
34. British Library Document Supply Centre **10**
35. British Library Lending Division **10**
36. British Library Reference Division **57**
37. British Medical Association Nuffield Library **4**
38. British Military Mission Durban **18; 168**
39. British Museum Natural History Library **139**
40. Bromley Public Library **229**
41. Buckfast Abbey Library **82**
42. Cambridge University Press Printers Library **235**
43. Cambridgeshire Libraries **256**
44. Camden Public Libraries **83**
45. Cardiff Public Libraries **190**
46. Carlisle Public Libraries **254**
47. Catholic Workers College Oxford **26**
48. Cawthorn, Hutt and Son Libraries **30**
49. Chatham House Library, Royal Institute of International Affairs **108**

50. Chelsea College of Science and Technology **90**
51. Chelsea Public Library **20**
52. Chelsea School of Art **107**

53. Cheltenham Public Library **233**
54. Churchill College, Cambridge **211**
55. City of London Libraries **135**
56. Clare College, Cambridge **231**
57. Coit Memorial Library, Queensway, London **237**
58. College of St Mark and St John **152**
59. College of St Mathias, Fishponds, Bristol **250**
60. Collegii Sancti Caroli Londini **64**
61. Command Lending Library, HQ BAOR **1**
62. Command Reference Library, Portsmouth Command **181**
63. Commonwealth Institute Library and Resource Centre **268**
64. Congregational Churches of Scotland **140**
65. Congregational College Manchester **132**
66. Conservative Research Department **137**
67. Convent of the Ladies of Mary, Scarborough **67**
68. Cornwall County Library **236**
69. Cornwall Technical College Library **111**
70. Corpus Christi College Junior Library, Oxford **6**
71. Crosby Public Libraries **48**
72. Coupland's Select Library, Clifton **218**
73. Coxley Lending Library **38**
74. Cunard Steamship Company Library **89**
75. Dagenham Public Libraries **206**
76. Daniel Stewart's College Library **192**
77. Dartford Public Libraries **129**
78. Day's Library, Mount Street, London **186**
79. Derbyshire County Library **127; 219**

80. Derbyshire County Library, New Mills **11**
81. Derbyshire Stone Ltd, Matlock **44**
82. Dettingen Officers Mess Library **205**
83. Devon and Exeter Institution **101**
84. Devon Library Services **187**
85. Douglas and Foulis, Edinburgh **171**
86. E.H. Easton Circulating Library, Plymouth **86**
87. Ealing Public Libraries **191**
88. East Wittering Congregational Church Library **155**
89. Edinburgh University Catholic Students Library **63**
90. Edlow's (private circulating library), Lancing, Sussex **253**
91. Elizabeth Gaskell College of Education **177**
92. Elsie Horder Memorial Library **193**
93. Emmanuel College, Cambridge **58**
94. Enfield College of Technology **273**
95. Erdington Public Libraries **39**
96. Exeter College, Oxford **32; 169**
97. Falkirk Public Libraries **196**
98. Ford Motor Company Ltd. Central Library **145**
99. Forest Library, Oxford **72**
100. Fort Dunlop Research Library **29**
101. Franciscan Convent, Goodings, nr. Newbury **258**
102. General Conference of the New Church **57**
103. Gonville and Caius College, Cambridge **43**
104. Grainthorpe Mutual Improvement Society Library **3**
105. GWR Mechanics Institution, Swindon **255**
106. Greater World Association **61**
107. Greenock Library Fairrie Bequest **115**
108. Greenwich Public Library **100**
109. Guildhall Library, London **73**
110. Hammersmith College of Art and Building **107**
111. Hammersmith Public Libraries **118**
112. Harrods Circulating Library **89**
113. Hastings Public Library **9; 74**
114. Hay Fleming Library, St Andrews **271**
115. Heinemann Staff Library **248**
116. HM Board of Customs and Excise Library, Intelligence Branch, Custom House **199**

117. HMS Raleigh Ship's Company Library **117**
118. HMS Rhyl Library **87**
119. HM Stationery Office **42**
120. Hertfordshire County Council Library **226**
121. Hertfordshire College of Further Education **94**
122. Hewett's Library and News Room, Upper Assembly Rooms Parade, Leamington **153**
123. Highgate Literary and Scientific Institution **208**
124. Holborn Public Libraries Central Library **93**
125. Holy Cross Abbey Stapehill Library **244**
126. Hope Trust, Edinburgh **238**
127. Imperial College London Haldane Library **68**
128. Imperial Yeomanry Library **14**
129. Ipswich Institute Library and Reading Room **103**
130. Ipswich Public Libraries **120**
131. Isle of Ely County Library **256**
132. Isle of Wight Institution **209**
133. Joint Services Staff College **243**
134. Junior Tradesmen's Regiment, Kinmel Park Camp **227**

FOUNDED

1758.

T<small>EL.</small>:

ROYAL 2636.

THE LIVERPOOL LIBRARY,
LYCEUM.

135. Kennard's Circulating Library, Merton Park, London **217**
136. King's College, Cambridge **62**
137. King's Libraries, London SW6 **150**
138. King's Own Scottish Borderers Club Library **102**
139. Lanark County Libraries **59**
140. Lancashire Library Rossendale **146**
141. Leeds Public Library **242**

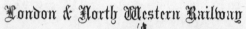

London & North Western Railway

LIBRARY AND LITERARY ASSOCIATION.

Euston Station.

NOTICE.

The attention of Members is directed to the very objectionable practice of writing or marking in the books and papers of the Association. With a view to checking this evil, it is requested that any member who may discover an apparently recent deface-ment, shall call the attention of the Librarian thereto, in order that the offender may be traced.

By order of the Committee.

Shelf
No.

Days⎰
Allowed⎱

This work must be returned within the specified time, unless renewed by application, and must not be transferred to any other Member without the sanction of the Librarian is first obtained.

142. Leicester University Library **24**
143. Lewin's Mead Congregational Library, Bristol **239**
144. Lexicon Libraries, Wells Road, Bristol Branch **223**
145. Library Association Library, Chaucer House **129**
146. Lincoln College, Oxford **119**

147. Little Gidding Library **40**
148. Liverpool Lyceum Library **225**
149. Parochial Library of Llanover in Monmouth **138**
150. London and NW Railway Library and Literary Association, Euston Station **95**
151. London County Council School of Building Library **247**
152. London School of Economics Shaw Library **241**
153. Loughborough College School of Librarianship **73**
154. Mackie Memorial Library, New Mills, Derby **11**
155. Magdalen College (Oxford) History Library **105**

156. City of Manchester College of Higher Education **51**
157. Manchester College of Housecraft **51**
158. Manchester Polytechnic Library **17; 51**
159. Marconi Company Library **281**
160. Marx Memorial Library **136**
161. Mather College Library **17**
162. Melchet Court Library, Silesian Theologate **160**
163. Middlesex Regiment 'B Company', 2nd Battalion **5**
164. Midland Railway Institute, Derby **30**
165. Mudie's Library **65**
166. National Assistance Board Library **130**
167. National Liberal Club Library **184**
168. Neville's Cross College, County of Durham **214**
169. New College, Oxford **183**
170. New Mills Public Library **11**

MARX
MEMORIAL LIBRARY

Without a revolutionary theory there cannot be a revolutionary movement

LENIN

PRESENTED BY —

_Pq_

CLASSIFICATION NO. ~~100~~ — 7828.

171. New Mills Technical Institute **11**
172. Newnham College Library, Cambridge **266**
173. Newton Park College, Bath **2**
174. Norfolk County Library **92**
175. North Devon Athenaeum, Barnstable **31**
176. Northumberland College **185**
177. Norwich City College Library **128**
178. Norwich Public Library **92**
179. Nuffield College, Oxford **144**
180. Office of Agent General for Ontario [Library] **96**
181. Oxford University Press Delegates Library **207**
182. Oxford University Press Printers Library **197**
183. Oxfordshire County Libraries **213**

184. Paddington Public Libraries **118**
185. Parsons Library, London House **134**
186. Pembroke College, Oxford **222**
187. Peninsular and Oriental Steam Navigation Company **182**
188. Perth Mechanics Library **46**
189. Philips Lamps Materials Research Laboratory **259**
190. Pitman House Reference Library **203**
191. Plessey Company Ltd. Technical Library **78**
192. Plymouth Public Library **53**
193. Pointer's Lending Library, Brighton **179**

194. Polytechnic of the South Bank **247**
195. Poplar Technical College Library **151**
196. The Priory, Hinckley **80**
197. Psychological Laboratory, Cambridge **270**
198. Queens' College, Cambridge **21**
199. The Queen's College, Oxford **109**
200. Rediffusion Television Reference Library **228**

201. Renfrew Public Library **141**
202. Richmond-upon-Thames Library Service **123**
203. College of Education, Ripon **178**

204. Rochester Society for the Cultivation of Useful
     Knowledge **272**
205. RAF Central Library and Book Depot, Upwood **10**
206. RAF College Library **7**
207. RAF Station Bodorgan Reference and Text book Library
     175
208. RAF Station Changi Reference and Text book Library **25**
209. RAF Station, Colerne, Sergeants Mess **232**
210. RAF White Waltham Station Reference and Textbook
     Library **60**
211. RAF Wyton, Hunts, Education Section Recreational
     Library **85**
212. Royal College of Nursing, Cavendish Square **97**
213. Royal Empire Society, Hove **260**
214. Royal Naval College, Greenwich **181**
215. Royal Naval College Osborne Cadets Library **45**
216. Royal Naval Engineering College Manadon Mess
     Library **116**
217. The Royal Society **99**
218. Saffron Waldon Training College Library **69**
219. St Aloysius, Oxford **163**
220. Saint Anne's Society Library, The Nettleship
     Collection **113**

221. St Clare's Hall, Oxford **220**
222. St Edmund Hall, Oxford **194**
223. St Hugh's College, Oxford **81**
224. St Ignatius', Preston **204**
225. St Luke's College Library **111**
226. St Martin-in-the-Fields Public Library **240**
227. St Mary Abbot's Hospital Patients Library **212**
228. St Mary's House Library **267**
229. St Marylebone Central Reference Library **110**
230. St Marylebone Free Public Library Association **75**
231. St Michael's Abbey, Farnborough **88**
232. St Thomas's Hospital Library **13**
233. Salford Royal Museum and Library, Peel Park **121**
234. Sandeman Public Library, Perth **104**
235. School of Infantry Library **174**
236. Scottish Office Library, Edinburgh **15; 142**
237. Seafarer's Education Service Crew's Library **270**
238. Seafarer's Education Service, London **265**
239. Seeley Historical Library, Cambridge **188**

240. Services Central Library **10**
241. Sheerness Dockyard Lending Library **189**
242. Sheffield Poetry Club Library **216**
243. Signet Library, Edinburgh **161**
244. Small Arms School Hythe Wing Reference Library **174**

245. Smedley's Hydro Matlock Library **215**
246. W.H. Smith & Sons Subscription Library **125**
247. Sneyd Park Subscription Library **219**
248. Ad Usum Scriptorum Societatis Jesu. Prov. Angl. **201**
249. Somerset County Library **133**
250. South Downs College of Further Education **16**
251. Southern Command Central Library **91**
252. Southwark Central Library **56**
253. Stepney Public Libraries **148**

SURBITON

PUBLIC
LIBRARY

254. Stoke Newington Public Libraries **110**
255. Sunderland Technical College Priestman Library **143**
256. Surbiton Public Library **159**
257. Sussex University Library **184**
258. The Sword and Shield Centre, Winchester **202**
259. G.E. Taylor Swindon [private lending library] **180**
260. Thorp's Subscription Library **157**
261. Tilbury Fort Military Library **50**
262. Torch Library **98**
263. Tower Hamlets Libraries **148**
264. United Universities Club Library **112**
265. University of Birmingham Library **156**
266. University of Bristol Library **33**
267. University of Bristol Medical Library **164**
268. University of Cambridge Extra-Mural Studies Library **263**
269. University of Exeter Catholic Society **8**
270. University of Exeter Institute of Education **47**
271. University of Glasgow Celtic Class Library **158**

272. University of Glasgow English Class Library **245**
273. University of Leeds Library **249**
274. University of Liverpool Institute of Education Library **264**
275. University of London Library **124; 154**
276. University of Reading Department of Politics Library **269**
277. Upper Norwood Public Library **122**
278. Victoria League Club Nutford House Library **126**
279. Wandsworth Public Libraries **257**
280. West Kent General Hospital Library **77**
281. City of Westminster Public Libraries **110**
282. Westminster College Library, Oxford **252**
283. Whitworth Institute, Darley Dale **41**
284. Wigan Free Public Library **262**
285. Wilmot Breeden Limited Operational Research Department **36**
286. Wiltshire Library and Museum Service **166; 224**
287. City of Winchester Public Library **54**
288. Worcester College, Oxford **109**
289. Worthing Public Library **70**
290. Yates Library, Kenton Park Parade **66**
291. Young's Lending Library, Regents Parade, Hayes **22**
292. Countess of Zetland's reading circle **162**

Sample List of Books Dispersed

The numbers after each title refer to the previous numbered list of libraries.

1. Alport, Lord: *The Sudden Assignment, Being a Record of Service in Central Africa during the Last Controversial Years of the Federation of Rhodesia and Nyasaland 1961-63* (1965) **61**
2. Altmayer, Arthur J.: *The Formative Years of Social Security* (1966) **173**
3. Andrews, William: *Bygone Lincolnshire* (1891) **104**
4. Archdall, Mervyn: *In Pursuit: A Selection of Editorial Writings* (1947), no. 6 of 150 copies signed by the author **37**
5. Army Bureau of Current Affairs: *War*, no. 38 (1943) **163**
6. Arnold, W.T.: *The Roman System of Provincial Administration* (1979) **70**
7. Ashworth, Wilfred: *Handbook of Special Librarianship and Information Work* (1955) **206**
8. Aspinall, A.: *The Cabinet Council 1783-1835* (1952) **269**
9. Aurelius, Marcus: *The XII Books of Marcus Aurelius Antoninus The Emperor* (1900) Limited Edition no. 148 of 325 copies **113**
10. Ausubel, Herman: *In Hard Times: Reformers amongst the Late Victorians* (1960) **34; 35; 205; 240**
11. Baird, Robert H: *The American Cotton Spinner and Managers' and Carders' Guide*, Philadelphia (1887) **80; 154; 170; 171**
12. Baird, Russell N.: See Turnbull, Arthur T. **59**
13. Baker, Michael H.C.: *Journey to Katmandu* (1974) **232**
14. Barham, Richard H.: *The Ingoldsby Legends* (1895) **128**

15. Barkan, Herbert and Konove, Carl: *Introduction to Mathematics with Applications* (1965) **207; 236**

16. Barker, Edward C.: *Psychology's Impact on the Christian Faith* (1964) **250**

17. [Penguin Modern Poets 3] *George Barker, Martin Bell, Charles Causley* (1962) **158; 161**

18. Barman, Christian: see Mawson, Christian [pseud] **23; 38**

19. Baumgarten, Franziska: *The Psychology of Human Relations in Industry* (1950) **31**

20. Beer, J.B.: *Coleridge the Visionary* (1959) **51**

21. Beerbower, James R.: *Search for the Past: An Introduction to Paleontology* (1960) **198**

22. Behrens, Margaret: *House of Dreams* (1932) **291**

23. Bell, Martin: see Barker, George **158; 161**

24. Benedict, Ruth: *Patterns of Culture* (1945) **142**

25. Benemy, F.W.G.: *Whitehall Town Hall* (1965) **208**

26. Benn, Ernest: *The State the Enemy* (1945) **47**

27. Bevan, Edwyn: *Holy Images: An Inquiry into Idolatry and Image-worship in Ancient Paganism and Christianity* (1940) **28**

28. Bigelow, Frank H.: *A Meteorological Treatise on the Circulation and Radiation in the Atmospheres of the Earth and the Sun* (1915) **159**

29. Birren, Faber: *Selling with Colour* (1945) **100**

30. Blennerhasset, Lady [Grafin Leydin]: *Talleyrand* (1894) **48; 164**

31. Bodley, John Edward Courtney: *Cardinal Manning. The Decay of Idealism in France. The Institute of France. Three Essays* (1912) **175**

32. Bolton, A.: see Merchant, W. **96**

33. Borkenau, Franz: *The Communist International* (1938) **266**

34. Bourne, H.R. Fox: *The Romance of Trade* (1871) **7**

35. Braybrooke, Patrick: *A Chesterton Catholic Anthology, compiled and edited by Patrick Braybrook* (1928) Inscribed by the Editor: 'To the Sacred Memory of G.K. Chesterton died June 14th 1936.' **8**

36. Brech, E.F.L. (ed.): *The Principles and Practice of Management* (1953) **285**

37. Bridgett, T.E.: *A History of the Holy Eucharist in Great Britain* (1908) **22**
38. Brightwell, C.L.: *Palissy, the Huguenot Potter: A True Tale* (1858) **73**
39. British Medical Association: *Secret Remedies* (1909) **95**
40. Brock, W.R.: *The Character of American History* (1965) **147**
41. Brooke, Stopford A.: *Tennyson: His Art and Relation to Modern Life* (1902) **283**
42. Brooks, Nelson: *Language and Language Learning Theory* (1960) **119**
43. Brunetaire, Ferdinand: *Histoire de la Littérature Française Classique* (1912) **103**
44. Bull, George and Vice, Anthony: *Bid for Power* (1958) **81**
45. Bullen, Frank T.: *A Bounty Boy, being some Adventures of a Christian Barbarian on an Unpremeditated Trip Round the World* (1907) **215**
46. Burke, Edmund: *The Works* (1945) **188**
47. Burt, Cyril (ed.): *How the Mind Works* (1948) **270**
48. Burton, S.H.: *The South Devon Coast* (1954) **71**
49. Bussell, Jan: *Through Wooden Eyes* (1956) **26; 27**
50. Cannon, Richard: *Historical Record of the Fourth or The King's Own Regiment of Foot* (1839) **261**
51. Cardus, Neville: *Close of Play* (1956) **134**
52. Causley, Charles: see Barker, George **158; 161**
53. Cecil, Henry: *Brief to Counsel* (1958) **192**
54. Cecil, Lord Hugh: *Conservatism* (1912) **287**
55. Chambers, Sir Edward: see Williams, Charles **274**
56. Chapman-Huston, Major Desmond (ed.): *Daisy Princess of Pless, by Herself* (1928) **252**
57. Child, Mrs D.L.: *The History of the Condition of Women* (1835) **36; 102**
58. Clarker, H. Butler: *Spanish Literature* (1921) **93**
59. Clough, Eric A.: *Bookbinding for Librarians* (1957) **139**
60. Clune, Frank: *High-Ho to London: Incidents and Interviews on a leisurely Journey by Air from Australia to Britain* (1948) **210**
61. Coates, James: *Seeing the Invisible: Practical Studies in Psychometry, Thought Transference, Telepathy and Allied*

Phenomena (1906) **106**

62. Collier, J. Payne: *Notes and Emendations to the Text of Shakespeare's Plays* (1852) **136**

63. Combe, William: *Doctor Syntax: His Three Tours in Search of The Picturesque, of Consolation, of a Wife* (n.d.) **89**

64. Cooper, Lane: *Aristotle on the Art of Poetry* (1913) **60**

65. Cranmer-Byng, L.: *The Vision of Asia* (1932) **165**

66. Croft-Cooke, Rupert: *Give Him the Earth* (1930) **290**

67. Cutts, Edward L.: *Scenes and Characters of the Middle Ages* (1926) **67**

68. Dalzell, William Ronald: *Architecture: The Indispensible Art* (1962) **127**

69. De Garmo, Charles: *Herbart and the Herbartarians* (1895) **218**

70. Dekker, Thomas: *[Various Works] Edited and with an Introduction by Ernest Rhys* (1949) **289**

71. Delmer, Sefton: *Black Boomerang* (1962) **25**

72. Department of Scientific and Industrial Research: *Soil Mechanics for Road Engineers* (1955) **99**

73. Dickson, William P.: *The Glasgow University Library: Notes on its History, Arrangements and Aims* (1888) **109; 153**

74. Djilas, Milovan: *Montenegro* (1964) **113**

75. Dobson, Austin: *Four Frenchwomen* (1890) **230**

76. Downey, Glanville: *Aristotle and Greek Science* (1964) **20**

77. Driberg, Tom: *Guy Burgess: A Portrait with Background* (1956) **280**

78. Drucker, Peter F.: *The New Society: The Anatomy of the Industrial Order* (1950) **191**

79. *Dumas' Art Annual 1882* (1882) **10**

80. Duncan, Martin: *Our Insect Friends and Foes* (1911) **196**

81. Duntzer, Heinrich: *The Life of Schiller* (1883) **223**

82. Durdent, R.J.: *Epoques et Faits Mémorables de l'Histoire de France* (1815) **41**

83. Dyer, James: *Southern England: An Archaeological Guide to the Prehistoric and Roman Remains* (1973) **44**

84. Evans, David Morier: *The City* (1845) **16**

85. Faulkner, William: *The Town* (1958) **211**

86. Ferguson, W.B.M.: *The Shayne Case* (1947) **86**

87. Finch, Mathew: *Eye with Mascara* (1968) **118**
88. Fodor, Eugene: *Fodor's Modern Guides: Germany* **231**
89. Ford, Ford Madox: *New York is not America* (1927) **74; 112**
90. Fox, E.A.: *Mechanics* (1967) **50**
91. Fraser, James [pseud]: *Deadly Nightshade* (1970) **5; 251**
92. Gallup, Donald: *T.S. Eliot: A Bibliography* (1952) **174; 178**
93. Gardner, Erle Stanley: *The Case of the Deadly Toy* (1964) **124**
94. Garnett, James Clerk Maxwell: *Education and World Citizenship: An Essay Towards a Science of Education* (1921) **11**
95. Mrs Gaskell: *Wives and Daughters* (1973) **150**
96. George, Henry: *Progress and Poverty* (1884) **180**
97. Gibbins, H. de B.: *Industry in England* (1915) **212**
98. Gibbs, Henry: *Disputed Barricade* (1952) **262**
99. [Gilbart, William James] *Logic for the Million: A Familiar Exposition of the Art of Reasoning* (1851). With stamp on title page: 'Soc. Regis. Lond. ex dono Auctoris' **217**
100. Gillard, Michael: *In the Name of Charity* (1987) **108**
101. Gissing, Algernon: *Baliol Garth* (1905) **83**
102. Gissing, George: *The Nether World* (1890) **138**
103. Gissing, George: *Will Warburton* (1905) **129**
104. Gladstone, W.E. (trans.): *The Odes of Horace* (1894). With bookplate: 'This work is presented to this institution with the compliments of Mr Gladstone's Trustees. Hawarden Castle, April, 1907.' **234**

This work is presented to this Institution with the compliments of Mr. Gladstone's Trustees.

HAWARDEN CASTLE,
April, 1907.

105. Green, John Richard: *A Short History of the English People* (1921) **155**

106. Greene, Graham: *Brighton Rock* (1952) **12**

107. Gresswell, Peter: *Houses in the Country* (1964) **52; 110**

108. Griffin, Keith: *Under-development in Spanish America* (1969) **49**

109. Halévy, Elie: *The Age of Cobden and Peel* (1947) **199; 288**

110. Halford, Sir Henry: *Essays and Orations* (1833) **229; 254; 281**

111. Hall, Calvin S.: *A Primer of Freudian Psychology* (1962) **69; 225**

112. Hall, Hubert (ed.): *List and Index of the Publications of the Royal Historical Society 1871-1924 and of the Camden Society 1840-1897* (1925) **264**

113. Hansen, Alvin H.: *Monetary Theory and Fiscal Policy* (1949) **220**

114. Harrison, John R.: *The Reactionaries, with a Preface by William Empson* (1966) **14**

115. Haydon, Frank Scott (ed.): *Eulogium Historiarum sive temporis: Chronicon ab Orbe condito Usque ad Annum M.CCC.LXVI a Monacho quodam Malmesburiensi exaratum* (1858) **107**

116. Highsmith, Patricia: *Those Who Walk Away* (1967) **216**

117. Hill, Vincent: *The Cunning Enemy* (1957) **117**

118. Hillson, Norman: *Geneva Scene* (1936) **111; 184**

119. Hilton, George W.: *The Truck System* (1960) **146**

120. Holland, Sir Henry: *Recollections of Past Life* (1872) **130**

121. Holman, H.: *Pestalozzi: An Acount of His Life and Work* (1908) **233**

122. Holtby, Winifred: *South Riding* (1979) **277**

123. Homberger, Eric (ed.): *The Cambridge Mind: Ninety Years of the Cambridge Review 1879-1969* (1970) **202**

124. Hudson, Derek, and Luckhurst, Kenneth W.: *The Royal Society of Arts 1754-1954* (1954) **275**

125. Hueffer, Francis: *Half a Century of Music in England 1837-1887. Essays towards a History* (1889) **246**

126. Hunt, Leigh: *Essays edited with an introduction and notes by Arthur Symons* (1888) **278**

127. Innes, Michael: *Carson's Conspiracy* (1984) **79**
128. Ionescu, Gita: *The New Politics of European Integration* (1972) **177**
129. Irwin, Raymond: British Bird Books: *An Index to British Ornithology A.D.1481 - A.D.1948* (1951) **77; 145**
130. Jenkins, Sir Gilmour: *The Ministry of Transport and Civil Aviation* (1959) **166**
131. Jenks, George C. and Moore, Carlyle: *Stop Thief!* New York (1913) **2**
132. Jones, Henry: *Idealism as a Practical Creed* (1909) **65**
133. Jordan, W.K.: *Edward VI: The Threshold of Power* (1970) Stamp on title page: 'Last Copy' **9; 249**
134. Joyce, James: *Portrait of the Artist as a Young Man* (1968) **185**
135. Jupp, James: *Political Parties* (1968) **55**
136. Kaltenborn, F.V.: *Kaltenborn Edits The News* (1937) **160**
137. *Keesing's Contemporary Archives* **66**
138. Kennett, Basil: *Romae Antiquae Notitia, or the Antiquities of Rome* (1699) **149**
139. Kenyon, Frederic G. (ed.): *The Poems of Bacchylides* (1897) [editio princeps] **33; 39**
140. Kern, H. (ed.): *The Saddharma-Pundarika* (1884) **64**
141. Kissinger, Henry A.: *A World Restored* (1973) **201**
142. Konove, Carl: see Barkan, Herbert **207; 236**
143. Kurihara, K. Kenneth: *Introduction to Keynesian Dynamics* (1958) **255**
144. Laski, Harold J.: *The Crisis and the Constitution: 1931 and After* (1932) **179**
145. Leger-Gordon, D. St.: *Devonshire* (1950) **98**
146. Leopold, Christopher: *The Night Fishers of Antibes* (1981) **140**
147. Leopold, Natah F.: *Life plus 99 Years, with an Introduction by Erle Stanley Gardner* (1958) **24**
148. Lewis, W.H.: *The Sunset of the Splendid Century: The Life and Times of Louis Auguste de Bourbon Duc de Maine 1670-1736* (1955) **253; 263**
149. Liepman, Hans Wolfgang and Puckett, Allen E.: *Introduction to Aerodynamics of a Compressible Fluid* (1948) **1**

150. Lodwick, John: *Contagion to this World* (1956) **137**

151. Longden, Edward: *Densening and Chilling in Foundry Work Ferrous and Non-Ferrous Casting* (1954) **195**

152. Lorenz, Konrad: *On Aggression* (1966) **58**

153. [Loudon, Mrs Jane C.] *The Mummy! A Tale of the Twenty-Second Century* (1828) **122**

154. Luckhurst, Kenneth W, see: Hudson, Derek **275**

155. MacArthur, Wilson: *The River Doon* (1952) **88**

156. McDougall, William: *Ethics and Some Modern World Problems* (1924) **265**

157. Macfall, Haldane: *The Wooings of Jezebel* (1913) **260**

158. Mackinnon, Donald: *A Descriptive Catalogue of Gaelic Manuscripts in the Advocates Library Edinburgh* (1912) **271**

159. Macmillan, Norman: *An Hour of Aviation* (1931) **256**

160. Madariaga, Salvador De: *The Fall of the Spanish American Empire* (1947) **162**

161. Madeley, Charles: *Catalogue of the Reference Library Warrington Municipal Museum* (1898) **243**

162. Maitland, S.R.: *The Dark Ages: A Series of Essays intended to Illustrate the State of Religion and Literature in the Ninth, Tenth, Eleventh and Twelfth Centuries* (1845) **292**

163. Mallock, W.H.: *Memoirs of Life and Literature* (1920) **219**

164. *Manual for Medical Staff Corps War Office* (1885) **267**

165. Marconi, Giuseppe: *Compendio Istorico della vita di S. Brigida Vedova Principessa Reale de Svezia* Rome (1789) **18**

166. Markov, Georgi and Phillips, David [pseud: St. George, David]: *The Right Honourable Chimpanzee* (1978) **286**

167. Marson, Una: *Towards the Stars* (1945) **29**

168. Mawson, Christian [pseud: Barman, Christian]: *Ramping Cat* (1941) **23; 38**

169. Merchant, W. and Bolton, A.: *An Introduction to the Theory of Structures* (1962) **96**

170. Meredith, George: *Evan Harrington* (1892) **19**

171. Merriman, Henry Seton: *Roden's Corner* (1898) **85**

172. Miller, Alexander: *The Christian Significance of Karl Marx* (1946) **3**

173. Miller, J.D.B.: *Australian Government and Politics* (1954) **6**

174. Millin, Sarah Gertrude: *General Smuts* (1936) **235; 244**
175. Montague, Sydney R.: *North to Adventure* (1939) **207**
176. Moore, Carlyle, see: Jenks, George C. **2**
177. Morris, William: *News from Nowhere* (1920) **91**
178. Morrish, Ivor: *Education Since 1800* (1970) **203**
179. Morton, H.V.: *In Search of England* (1939) **193**
180. Moseley, Maboth: *This Lady was a Gentleman* (1931) **180**
181. Mowat, Charles Loch: *Britain between the Wars 1918-1940* (1955) **62; 214**
182. Murray, Hugh: *The Travels of Marco Polo* (1845) **187**
183. Myres, J.L.: *A History of Rome* (1920). This volume bears the following bookplate: 'Hunc librum usitatum diu et dilectum Professoris Wykehamici perfunctus officio studiosis inceptantibus tradidit IOANNES LINTON MYERS Collegii Novi Socius MCMXXXIX' **169**

O.5031.

HUNC LIBRUM
USITATUM DIU ET DILECTUM
PROFESSORIS WYKEHAMICI
PERFUNCTUS OFFICIO
STUDIOSIS INCEPTANTIBUS
TRADIDIT
IOANNES LINTON MYRES
COLLEGII NOVI SOCIUS
MCMXXXIX

184. Namasivaayam, S.: *The Legislatures of Ceylon 1928-1948* (1951) **167; 257**

185. Nanda, B.R.: *The Nehrus, Motilal and Jawaharlal* (1965) **176**

186. Newborough, Lady: *The Memoirs of Mary Stella (Lady Newborough)* (1914) **78**

187. Newby, P.H.: *Kith* (1977) **84**

188. Newton, Eric: *An Introduction to European Painting* (1949) **239**

189. Nicols, Arthur: *The Puzzle of Life* (1877) **241**

190. Norman, Frank: *Too Many Crooks Spoil the Caper* (1979) **45**

191. O'Higgins, Paul: *Censorship in Britain* (1972) **87**

192. Oliver, J.W.: *The Life of William Beckford* (1937). With bookplate: 'Bequeathed by Mrs Jessie Meikle, widow of Henry W. Meikle, Keeper of the National Library and Historiographer Royal.' **76**

193. Oppenheim, E. Phillips: *The Great Impersonation* (1946) **92**

194. Owen, David: *The Politics of Defence* (1972) **222**

195. Pannikar, K.M.: *The Relation of Indian States with the Government of India* (1927) **4**

196. Parke, N.G.: *Guide to the Literature of Mathematics and Physics* (1947) **97**

197. Patmore, Coventry: *Courage in Politics and other Essays* (1921) **182**

198. Pearson, John: *An Exposition of the Creed* (1830) **30**

199. Peel, Mrs S.C.: *How We Lived Then, 1914-1918: A Sketch of Social and Domestic Life During the War* (1929) **116**

200. Phillips, David: see Markov, Georgi **286**

201. Piatt, John James: *Little New-World Idylls* (1893) **248**

202. Piddington, W.E.R.: *Russian Frenzy* (1955) **258**

203. Pitman, Isaac: *Dictionary of Commercial Correspondence* (1917) **190**

204. Pollen, J.H.: *The Life and Letters of Father John Morris* (1896) **224**

205. Polson Newman, Major E.W.: *Italy's Conquest of Abyssinia* (1937) **82**

206. Pond, Hugh: *Salerno* (1961) **13; 75**
207. Postgate, John Percival (ed.): *Tibulli Aliorumque Carminum Tres* (1939) **181**
208. Powell, Lawrence Clark: *A Passion for Books* (1959) **123**
209. Prideux, Humphrey: *The True Nature of Imposture Displayed in the Life of Mahomet* (1723) **132**
210. Puckett, Allen E.: see Liepman, Hans Wolfgang **1**
211. Quadling, D.A.: *Mathematical Analysis* (1955) **54**
212. Quennell, Peter: *John Ruskin: The Portrait of a Prophet* (1949) **227**
213. Quennell, Peter (ed.): *Memoirs of William Hickey* (1960) **183**
214. Read, Herbert: *Form in Modern Poetry* (1948) **168**
215. Reade, Charles: *The Cloister and the Hearth* (1873) **245**
216. Renshaw, C.A.: *Narcotics* (1923) **242**
217. Roberts, Morley: *Bianca's Caprice* (1904) **135**
218. Roberts, Morley: *The Colossus: A Story of Today* (1899) **72**
219. Roberts, Morley: *The Colossus: A Story of Today* (1899) **247**
220. Robinson, E.A.G.: *The Structure of Competitive Industry* (1960) **221**
221. Ross, Sir John: *Narrative in Search of a North-West Passage* (1835) **21**
222. *Royal Commission on the Press 1947-1949* (1949) **186**
223. Sackville-West, V: *Grand Canyon* (1942) **144**
224. St George [pseud]: see Markov, Georgi **286**
225. St John, Bayle: *Montaigne the Essayist* (1858) **148**
226. Sartre, Jean-Paul: *Nekrasov* (1956) **120**
227. Savage, George: *The Antique Collector's Handbook* (1960) **135**
228. Schramm, Wilbur (ed.): *The Impact of Educational Television* (1960) **200**
229. Scott, Eva: *The Travels of the King: Charles II in Germany and Flanders 1654-1660* (1907) **40**
230. Scott, Sir Walter: *Tales of a Grandfather* (1830) **17**
231. Seaman, Owen: *Horace at Cambridge* (1895) **56**
232. Seth, Ronald: *The Spy Who Wasn't Caught* (1966) **209**
233. Shahn, Ben: *The Shape of Content* (1957) **53**

234. Sharp, Evelyn: *The Ministry of Housing and Local Government* (1969) **15**

235. Sherrington, Sir Charles: *Man on His Nature* (1953) **42**

236. Siegfried, André: *England's Crisis* (1933) **68**

237. Smith, G. Elliot: *Human Nature* (1927) **57**

238. Smith, Horace and James: *Rejected Addresses or the New Theatrum Poetarum* (1813) **126**

239. Solly, Henry: *The Great Atonement* (1847) **143**

240. Sotheby, S. Leigh: *Ramblings in the Elucidation of the Autograph of Milton* (1896) **226**

241. Spark, Muriel: *Voices at Play* (1961) **152**

242. Speaight, Robert: *Teilhard de Chardin* (1967) **141**

243. Spear, Percival: *India, Pakistan and the West* (1949) **133**

244. Stanhope, Walter: *Monastic London* (1887) **125**

245. Stevenson, Robert Louis: *Underwoods* (1887) **272**

246. Stewart, J. I.M.: see Innes, Michael [pseud] **79**

247. Swarbrick, John: *Easements of Light: Modern Methods of Computing Compensation* (1937?) **151; 194**

248. Thorne, Anthony: *Fruit in Season* (1938) **115**

249. Tonge, Thomas: *Heraldic Visitation of the Northern Counties in 1530* (1863) **273**

250. Turnbull, Arthur T. and Baird, Russell N.: *The Graphics of Communication* (1968) **59**

251. Vice, Anthony: see Bull, George **81**

252. Ward, Adolphus William (ed.): *Marlow's Tragical History of Dr. Faustus* (1901) **282**

253. Warner, Rex: *The Young Caesar* (1958) **90**

254. Watkin, E.I.: *Roman Catholicism in England from the Reformation to 1950* (1957) **32; 46**

255. Watson, John Selby: *The Life of Porson* (1862) **105**

256. Watson, Sir William: *The Poems 1878-1935* (1936) **43; 131**

257. Waugh, Alec: *The Best Wine Last: An Autobiography Through the Years 1932-1969* (1978) **279**

258. Wessely, J.E.: *A New Pocket Dictionary of the English and Italian Languages* (n. d.) **101**

259. Weston, H.C.: *Sight, Light and Efficiency* (1949) **189**

260. Weyman, Stanley: *From the Memoirs of a Minister of France* (1909) **213**

261. White, Alan: see Fraser, James [pseud] **5**; **251**
262. *Wigan Free Public Library: Its Rise and Progress: A List of its Treasures; With an Account of the Twenty-First Anniversary of its Opening* (1901) **284**
263. Wilhelm, Donald: *The West Can Win* (1966) **268**
264. Williams, Charles and Chambers, Sir Edmund: *A Short Life of Shakespeare with the Sources* (1950) **274**
265. Wilsher, Peter: *The Pound in Your Pocket 1870-1970* (1970) **238**
266. Wilson, Charles Heath: *Life and Works of Michelangelo Buonarotti* (1876) **172**
267. Wilson Knight, G.: *The Dynasty of Stowe* (1945) **228**
268. Winstedt, Sir Richard (ed.): *Indian Art* (1947) **63**
269. Wiseman, H.V. : *Political Systems: Some Sociological Approaches* (1966) **276**
270. Wood Jones, Frederick: *Design and Purpose* (1943) **167**; **237**
271. Wyatt, Woodrow: *Southwards from China* (1952) **114**
272. Yerby, Frank: *Captain Rebel* (1958) **204**
273. Zweig, Ferdinand: *The Student in the Age of Anxiety* (1963) **94**

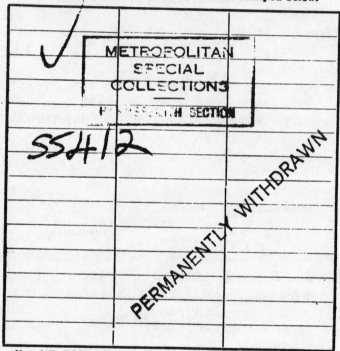

HAMMERSMITH PUBLIC LIBRARIES
LENDING DEPARTMENTS

CENTRAL (CARNEGIE) LIBRARY

(Telephone No. : RIVerside 5018)

The time allowed for reading this book is fourteen days, and it is due for return (to the Library from which it was issued) not later than the last date stamped below.

Notes

1. Lord Quinton, 'Who shall Survive?' in *Conservation and Collection Management: Proceedings of a Seminar at Loughborough University of Technology 22-23 July 1987*, National Preservation Office, The British Library (1988) ['Seminar'], p. 9.

2. Bob Duckett in *Librarian Association Record* [*LAR*] (June 1990), p. 435.

3. John Pateman in *LAR* (July 1990), p. 491.

4. Bob Duckett in *LAR* (September 1990), p. 663. Mr Duckett, Senior Librarian at Bradford Libraries and Information Service, wrote two articles on book dispersal and library management. His opinions appear to have developed in the interval between the two.

5. Bob Duckett in *LAR* (June 1990), p. 433.

6. John Pateman, op. cit.

7. Bob Duckett in *LAR* (June 1990), p. 433.

8. Thomas Greenwood, *Public Libraries* (1891), p. xxiii.

9. Ibid., 332.

10. An interesting example found in the British Library report is S3RBK. This refers to a group of Universities engaged on a project and stands for their initials, S3 because the first three begin with S thus: Surrey, Sussex, Southampton, and then Reading, Brunel and Kent.

11. David Liddle in 'Seminar', p. 33.

12. Richard Hoggart, *Independent on Sunday,* 30 June 1991.

13. J.T. Gillett in *LAR* (August 1990), p. 568.

14. *LAR* (September 1990), p. 650.

15. Ian Morson, sometime Head of Stock Services at Brent Library, *LAR* (December 1990), p. 908.

16. Lorraine Williams in *LAR* (September 1990), p. 667.

17. David Liddle in 'Seminar', p. 33.

18. Bob Duckett in *LAR* (September 1990), p. 664.

19. I am grateful to Mr John Birch, Librarian at the Department of Education and Science, for the information supplied here.

20. David Vaisey in 'Seminar', p. 53.

21. Lord Quinton in 'Seminar', p. 8.

22. As cited in Ernest A. Savage, *The Story of Libraries and Book-Collecting* (1909), p. 132.

Index

Annapolis, Bray library in, 28
Archer, Jeffrey, 23, 57
Association of Independent Libraries, 31
Athenaeum Club, 26
Avon County Council, 31
Avon County Libraries, 27, 41
Ayr, 10

Bath Royal Literary and Scientific Institution, 29
BBC, 7, 8, 19, 53-5
BBC Enterprises, 7
BBC Library, 7
BBC Written Archive Centre, Caversham, 7, 20
Bentley, Richard, 51
Bible, First Book of Corinthians, 56
Blair, Eric Arthur, see Orwell, George
Bloomsbury, 51
Bloomsbury Book Auctions, 42
Bodleian Library, 46, 48
Bodley, Sir Thomas, 46
Boer War, 32
Boots Booklovers Library, 32-3
Bray, the Reverend Dr, 28-9
Bredon Reading Society, 29
Brent Library, 8, 12, 14, 34, 38, 40-1, 50
Brent Show, 40
Brentford, 10, 54
Brighton, 12
Bristol, 12
British Library, 8, 20, 37, 48-9, 50-1, 58
British Library Act, 27
British Library Board, 8
Burger King Restaurants, 33
Burgess, Guy, 8
Burt, Cyril, 53
The Butts, Brentford, 54

Cambridge, 12, 25
Carnegie, Andrew, 10, 38, 54
Churchill, Winston Spencer, 22
Civil War (English), 45
Conservative Party, 20-1
Conservative Party Central Office, 22, 57
Conservative Party Research Department, 21-2, 51

Dainton, Lord, 36, 51
Day's Circulating Library, 33-4, 36
Dell, Ethel M, 31-2
Delmer, Sefton, 54
Derby, 12
Derbyshire County Council, 37
Devon, 10, 29
Devon and Exeter Institution, 29
The Diary of Laura Palmer, 56
Disraeli, Benjamin, 22-3
Dobbs, Michael, 23, 57
Dominic Winter Book Auctions, 42
Donne, John, 56
Dust-jacket design, 49, 50

Ealing Public Library, 32
Edinburgh, 12
Exeter, 12, 32

Franklin, Benjamin, 29
First World War, 32
'Face-on' display, 16, 24
Freedom of Information Act, 44

Gillet, J. T., 38-9
Gissing, George, 32
Gladstone, William Ewart, 10, 18, 19, 20, 23, 33, 36
Glasgow, 25
Greenhamism, 39
Greenwood, Thomas, 10
Guildhall Library, 25

Harris, Thomas, 56
Harrods Library, 33
Henry VIII, King, 45
Hereford Cathedral, 45
Herts, 40
Hillingdon Report, 39
Hoggart, Richard, 33, 36-7
Hunslet, Leeds, 33

Ipswich Institute, 29
Isle of Wight Institution, 29

John Ryland's Library, 31

Kaltenborn, H. V., 54
Karl Marx Memorial Library, 54
Keesings Contemporary Archives, 22
Kent, 43
Keynes, John Maynard, 46
King's Libraries, The, 51
Knights Templar, 45

Langham Hotel, 7
Librarianship, radical, 39
Library Association, 13
Library Association Record, 9, 38-9
Liddle, David, 27, 41, 48
Linfield, Alan M.,40
The Listener, 54-5
London, 12, 25, 48
London Library, 31
Loughborough, 25
Loughborough School of Librarianship, 25
Loughborough Seminar, 8, 27, 48

Mackie Memorial Library, 37-8
Manchester, 31
Mappa Mundi, 45
Marson, Una, 7, 8, 54
Marylebone Public Library, 14
McDonald's Restaurants, 33
Middlesex, 54
Mills and Boon, 32
Milton Keynes, 54
Mudie's Lending Library, 32

National Socialist (Nazi) Party of Germany, 40
New College, Oxford, 25-6
New Mills Heritage Centre, 37-8
New Mills Library, 8, 14, 54
New Mills Technical Institute, 37

Official Secrets Act, 44
Open University, 53-5
Orwell, George (pseud Eric Arthur Blair), 7, 21, 31
Oxbridge (i.e. Oxford and/or Cambridge), 47-8
Oxford, 12, 25, 51

Patten, Christopher, 21-3
People's Convention, 50
People's Universities (i.e. the Public Libraries), 32-3, 36
Pluto Press, 39
Public Library Acts, 42
Public Record Office, 7, 20

Quinton, Lord, 8, 9, 48

Reformation, 45-6
Roberts, Morley, 32
Rochester, 12

Saatchi and Saatchi, 23
Sackville Street, 7
St. Edward Hall, Oxford, 25
St. Martin-in-the-Fields Public Library, 18
Sheerness Dockyard Library, 29
Sheffield, 36
Sheffield Public Library, 36
Shelley, Mary, 56
The Silence of the Lambs (by Thomas Harris), 56
Smith, W. H., 10, 18-i9
Sothebys Taunton, 22
Spark, Muriel, 54
Stalin, Joseph, 40-1, 54
Story, Jack Trevor, 34
Swindon, 12

TV 'Tie-in' Books, 23, 55, 57
Thackeray, William Makepeace, 23
Thatcher, Mrs Margaret, 20-2, 46, 51, 57-8
Times Lending Library, 33
Tring, 40
Trinity College, Cambridge, 51
Twin Peaks (TV Series), 56

Vaisey, David, 27
Video industry, videos, 57
Voice (Broadcast Poetry Magazine), 54

Westminster, 36
Westminster Library, 22, 41
Wilkes, John, 54
Willesden Green, 38-9

Zetland, Lady, Reading Circle of, 29

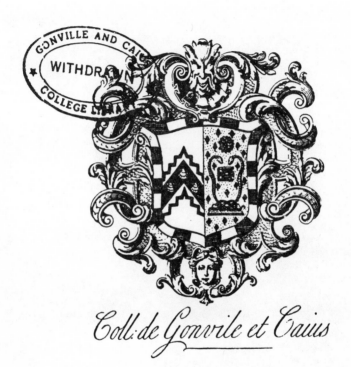

Coll: de Gonvile et Caius